Complex Operational Decision Making in Networked Systems of Humans and Machines

A Multidisciplinary Approach

NATIONAL RESEARCH COUNCIL
OF THE NATIONAL ACADEMIES

COMPLEX OPERATIONAL DECISION MAKING IN NETWORKED SYSTEMS OF HUMANS AND MACHINES

A MULTIDISCIPLINARY APPROACH

Committee on Integrating Humans, Machines and Networks:
A Global Review of Data-to-Decision Technologies

Board on Global Science and Technology

Policy and Global Affairs

NATIONAL RESEARCH COUNCIL
OF THE NATIONAL ACADEMIES

THE NATIONAL ACADEMIES PRESS
Washington, D.C.
www.nap.edu

THE NATIONAL ACDEMIES PRESS   500 Fifth Street, NW   Washington, DC 20001

NOTICE: The project that is the subject of this report was approved by the Governing Board of the National Research Council, whose members are drawn from the councils of the National Academy of Sciences, the National Academy of Engineering, and the Institute of Medicine. The members of the committee responsible for the report were chosen for their special competences and with regard for appropriate balance.

This study was supported by Contract/Grant No. 101380-Data-to-Decisions between the National Academy of Sciences and the Department of the Army. Any opinions, findings, conclusions, or recommendations expressed in this publication are those of the author(s) and do not necessarily reflect the views of the organizations or agencies that provided support for the project.

International Standard Book Number 13: 978- 0-309-30770-3
International Standard Book Number 10: 0-309-30770-8

Additional copies of this report are available from the National Academies Press, 500 Fifth Street, NW, Room 360, Washington, DC 20001; (800) 624-6242 or (202) 334-3313; http://www.nap.edu

Copyright 2014 by the National Academy of Sciences. All rights reserved.

Printed in the United States of America

THE NATIONAL ACADEMIES
Advisers to the Nation on Science, Engineering, and Medicine

The **National Academy of Sciences** is a private, nonprofit, self-perpetuating society of distinguished scholars engaged in scientific and engineering research, dedicated to the furtherance of science and technology and to their use for the general welfare. Upon the authority of the charter granted to it by the Congress in 1863, the Academy has a mandate that requires it to advise the federal government on scientific and technical matters. Dr. Ralph J. Cicerone is president of the National Academy of Sciences.

The **National Academy of Engineering** was established in 1964, under the charter of the National Academy of Sciences, as a parallel organization of outstanding engineers. It is autonomous in its administration and in the selection of its members, sharing with the National Academy of Sciences the responsibility for advising the federal government. The National Academy of Engineering also sponsors engineering programs aimed at meeting national needs, encourages education and research, and recognizes the superior achievements of engineers. Dr. C. D. Mote, Jr., is president of the National Academy of Engineering.

The **Institute of Medicine** was established in 1970 by the National Academy of Sciences to secure the services of eminent members of appropriate professions in the examination of policy matters pertaining to the health of the public. The Institute acts under the responsibility given to the National Academy of Sciences by its congressional charter to be an adviser to the federal government and, upon its own initiative, to identify issues of medical care, research, and education. Dr. Harvey V. Fineberg is president of the Institute of Medicine.

The **National Research Council** was organized by the National Academy of Sciences in 1916 to associate the broad community of science and technology with the Academy's purposes of furthering knowledge and advising the federal government. Functioning in accordance with general policies determined by the Academy, the Council has become the principal operating agency of both the National Academy of Sciences and the National Academy of Engineering in providing services to the government, the public, and the scientific and engineering communities. The Council is administered jointly by both Academies and the Institute of Medicine. Dr. Ralph J. Cicerone and Dr. C. D. Mote, Jr., are chair and vice chair, respectively, of the National Research Council.

www.national-academies.org

Committee on Integrating Humans, Machines and Networks: A Global Review of Data-to-Decision Technologies

Honorable Jacques S. Gansler (*Chair*)
> Professor & Roger C. Lipitz Chair, Director, Center for Public Policy and Private Enterprise, School of Public Policy, University of Maryland, College Park, MD

Mary (Missy) Cummings
> Associate Professor, Mechanical Engineering & Materials Science, Duke University, Durham, NC

Barbara J. Grosz,
> Higgins Professor of Natural Sciences, School of Engineering and Applied Sciences, Harvard University, Cambridge, MA

Anita Jones, University Professor Emerita, Department of Computer Science, University of Virginia, Charlottesville, VA

Amy A. Kruse
> Vice President, Intific, Inc., Alexandria, VA

George R. Mangun
> Dean of Social Sciences, Professor of Neurology and Psychology, University of California, Davis, Davis, CA

Tom Mitchell
> E. Fredkin University Professor, Chair, Machine Learning Department, School of Computer Science, Carnegie Mellon University, Pittsburgh, PA

See-Kiong Ng
> Program Director, Urban Systems Initiative, Institute for Infocomm Research (Singapore), Associate Professor, Singapore University of Technology and Design, Singapore

Donald A. Norman
> Nielsen Norman Group, Prof. Emeritus, Computer Science, Northwestern University, Prof. Emeritus, Cognitive Science and Psychology, University of California, San Diego, Palo Alto, CA

Guillermo R. Sapiro
> Professor, Department of Electrical and Computer Engineering, Duke University, Durham, NC

Ross D. Shachter
> Associate Professor of Management Science and Engineering, Department of Management Science and Engineering, Stanford University, Stanford, CA

James D. Shields
> President and CEO, Charles Stark Draper Laboratory, Cambridge, MA

Liz Sonenberg
> Professor, Department of Computing and Information Systems, and Pro Vice-Chancellor for Research Collaboration, Department of Computing and Information Systems, The University of Melbourne, Melbourne, Australia

Katia Sycara
> Research Professor, School of Computer Science, Carnegie Mellon University, Pittsburgh, PA

Alyson Wilson
> Associate Professor, Department of Statistics, North Carolina State University, Raleigh, NC

Victor Zue
> Director of International Relations, Computer Science and Artificial Intelligence Laboratory, Delta Electronics Professor, Electrical Engineering & Computer Science, Massachusetts Institute of Technology, Cambridge, MA (Committee member through April 3, 2013)

Project Staff

William O. Berry, Board Director
Ethan N. Chiang, Program Officer (through May 2, 2014)
Neeraj Gorkhaly, Research Associate (through February 21, 2014)
Peter Hunsberger, Financial Officer (through March 14, 2014)
Evelyn Strauss, Consultant Writer
Patricia S. Wrightson, Study Director
Scott Weidman, Director, Board on Mathematical Sciences and Their Applications, Advisor and Technical Editor to the study

Board on Global Science and Technology

Ruth David (*Chair*), President and CEO, Analytic Services, Inc., Falls Church, VA
Jeffrey Bradshaw, Florida Institute for Human and Machine Cognition, Pensacola, FL
Dianne Chong, Vice President, The Boeing Company, Bellevue, WA
Nan Jokerst, Department of Electrical and Computer Engineering, Duke University, Durham, NC
Bernard Meyerson, Vice President, IBM Corporation, Yorktown Heights, NY
Neela Patel, Director, External Research, Global Pharmaceutical R&D, Abbott Laboratories, Belmont, CA
Daniel Reed, Vice President for Research and Economic Development, University of Iowa, Iowa City, IA

Board Staff
William O. Berry, Board Director
Patricia S. Wrightson, Associate Board Director
Ethan N. Chiang, Program Officer (through May 2, 2014)
Neeraj Gorkhaly, Research Associate (through February 21, 2014)
Peter Hunsberger, Financial Officer (through March 14, 2014)

Preface and Acknowledgments

How might computational systems improve decision making in complex situations? This question prompted the National Ground Intelligence Center of the U.S. Army to sponsor a multidisciplinary and global assessment of the technologies that might help turn data into better decisions. The committee was tasked with studying the several technologies relevant to the topic; reviewing research in these areas conducted inside and outside of the United States; and then integrating those understandings into a multidisciplinary, global, and future-oriented assessment of human-machine collaboration for complex decision making.

The committee was multidisciplinary, representing numerous areas of expertise in the natural, physical, and social sciences that have a stake in human-machine collaboration for complex decision making. Although necessary for a project of this scope, this diversity provided additional complexity, as the committee members did not share a lexicon or common understanding of these issues. In the future, a project of this sort would greatly benefit from building a shared vocabulary and understanding of issues.

Given these practical and intellectual constraints, the report does not constitute the in-depth technical study that was initially planned. It does offer, however, a valuable assessment of the opportunities and challenges posed by research into human-machine collaboration for decision making, along with suggestions for further research. There is no doubt that continued advances in software, algorithms, representations, hardware, and understanding about the brain and human behavior over the next few decades will make this area of inquiry more relevant, not only to "how" we decide, but indeed, how we live.

This report has been reviewed in draft form by individuals chosen for their diverse perspectives and technical expertise, in accordance with procedures approved by the National Academies' Report Review Committee. The purpose of this independent review is to provide candid and critical comments that will assist the institution in making its published report as sound as possible and to ensure that the report meets institutional standards for objectivity, evidence, and responsiveness to the study charge. The review comments and draft manuscript remain confidential to protect the integrity of the process.

We wish to thank the following individuals for their review of this report: George Bekey, University of Southern California; Jeffrey Bradshaw, Florida Institute for Human and Machine Cognition; Joseph Gray, Oregon Health & Science University; Eric Horvitz, Microsoft Research; Sara Kiesler, Carnegie Mellon University; Peter Norvig, Google Inc.; Robert Sloan, University of Illinois at Chicago; and David Woods, Ohio State University.

Although the reviewers listed above have provided many constructive comments and suggestions, they were not asked to endorse the conclusions or recommendations, nor did they see the final draft of the report before its release. The review of this report was overseen by Robert Sproull, Oracle Labs (Retired). Appointed by the National Academies, he was responsible for making certain that an independent examination of this report was carried out in accordance with institutional procedures and that all review comments were carefully considered. Responsibility for the final content of this report rests entirely with the authoring committee and the institution.

My thanks go to the committee and staff for all of their efforts.

Sincerely,

Jacques Gansler, Chair
Committee on Integrating Humans, Machines and Networks: A Global Review
of Data-to-Decision Technologies

CONTENTS

SUMMARY — 1

CHAPTER 1 INTRODUCTION — **5**

CHAPER 2 COMPUTING AND DECISION MAKING TODAY — **11**
OVERVIEW OF DECISION MAKING, 12
BIG DATA, 17
FROM TOOLS TO TEAMMATES, 20

CHAPTER 3 HUMAN ELEMENTS OF TEAM DECISION MAKING — **23**
DECISION ANALYSIS, 23
HUMAN TEAMWORK, 25
COMMUNICATION: ESSENTIAL AND CHALLENGING, 26
TRUST, 27
HUMAN COGNITION AND MEMORY, 29
ERRORS IN HUMAN JUDGMENT AND DATA, 32
TASK ALLOCATION, 34

CHAPTER 4 MACHINE AND NETWORK ELEMENTS OF TEAM DECISION MAKING — **37**
MIXED HUMAN-COMPUTER TEAMS, 37
SYSTEM BRITTLENESS AND RESILIENT SYSTEMS, 39
DATA ANALYTICS, 41
DISTRIBUTED NETWORKS, 43
FLEXIBLE HUMAN-MACHINE INTERACTION, 44
METRICS, 45

CHAPTER 5 ENABLING TECHNOLOGIES — **49**
SENSING, 49
SOFTWARE AGENTS. 51
    AGENTS SUPPORTING HUMANS , 52
    RESEARCH CHALLENGES IN AGENT SUPPORT 53
NEUROSCIENCE, 54
HUMAN COMPUTATION, 57

CHAPTER 6 CONCLUSION — **61**

APPENDIXES

APPENDIX A COMMITTEE BIOGRAPHIES   **65**

APPENDIX B INTERNATIONAL VISITS   **73**
SINGAPORE, APRIL 15-19, 2013, 74
GERMANY, AUGUST 1-3, 2013, 76

APPENDIX C REFERENCES   **79**

SUMMARY

Over the past 2 decades, computing and communications networks have made it possible for decision makers to access enormous amounts of information. Entire libraries are available for searching, multiple streams of sensed data may be tapped, and collections of other network users can in many cases be accessed readily. Machine learning and natural language processing have advanced to the point where they can often provide basic pre-processing of diverse types of data. Computational support in the form of large-scale data collection and analysis, visualization, etc. has been readily incorporated into some human decision making processes. For example, computation is in the control processes for all manner of processing plants (chemical processing, nuclear power generation and petroleum refining), infrastructure (electric grid and telecommunications), manufacturing (chip fabrication and large scale baking plants), assembly (electronics and automotive robotic assembly), transactions (credit card and banking) and the military (management of theater operations).

However, the ease with which humans have already integrated computational systems into decision making ranging from ordinary to critical, from simple to complex, belies a deeper truth: this area of inquiry is still in its infancy relative to where multi-disciplinary research could take it over the next generation. This state of affairs has generated an environment that is ripe for a re-thinking of human-computer collaboration in the context of complex decision making. The vast amount of information that can be brought to bear does not guarantee better decisions or a more straightforward or reliable decision-making process. How to take advantage of these capabilities is the subject of this report of the Committee on Integrating Humans, Machines and Networks: A Global Review of Data-to-Decision Technologies.

The multidisciplinary committee that was formed at the request of the National Ground Intelligence Center of the U.S. Army (NGIC) included experts in autonomous agents, cognitive science, decision analysis, machine learning, neuroscience, statistics, and other areas. The sponsor wanted to better understand how enabling technologies are being integrated to inform and improve computer-assisted decision making; what some of the impediments are to their integration; and obtain a sense of the research that is occurring in university, government, and industrial labs inside and outside of the United States.

Early on in its deliberations, the committee perceived the unbounded nature of this broad topic—that is, the more they learned as a group about the varied aspects of human-machine collaboration for decision making, the more there was to study. Thus the committee concluded that a useful contribution to this topic at this time would be a preliminary exploration of the issues that could provide a roadmap for future multidisciplinary research. The report's structure takes a linear path: from human decision making; to relevant new computing capabilities; to emerging explorations of human-computer team decision making; to several research challenges that need to be overcome in order to realize the next steps in human-machine collaboration for complex decision making.

Following are the committee's findings. They are listed in the order that they appear in the text:

Finding 1: A common representation of the decision-making process, used to train fighter pilots in rapid decision making for air combat, calls for sequential steps to observe, update beliefs, choose an action, and take the action (the so-called OODA loop). While those steps are inherent to any careful decision making, for complex decisions the OODA loop framework does not readily reflect feedback loops between the steps and branching to consider multiple choices of action, both of which are common. The study of decision making in complex situations, and the design of automated decision support systems, requires an understanding of those complexities. Thus the OODA-loop framework may not be sufficient in those contexts.

Finding 2: Increasingly the data used to support computer-assisted decisions are drawn from heterogeneous sources (e.g. unstructured text, images, simulation outputs). Current techniques for filtering and aggregating these disparate data types into a well-characterized input for decision making are limited, which therefore limits the quality of the decisions.

Finding 3: While improved information availability can improve the quality of decision making, more information alone is not sufficient. This is particularly evident in complex scenarios where the goals of different team members are not completely aligned and delays make it difficult to attribute effects to actions.

Finding 4: Computer assists to human decision making will "come of age" when some of the computational elements are not simply assistive, but perform at a level that they are trusted as "near-peer" teammates in an integrated human-computer system. One of the key challenges of this integration will be the development of new techniques for test and evaluation that build trust between the human partner and the computational elements.

Finding 5: Humans and computation have different strengths in what they accomplish and there are several aspects of human decision making that can benefit from computer-aided systems, such as cognition, recognition of errors in judgment and task allocation. Similarly, there are several aspects of computer processing that can benefit from human guidance, such as prioritization, dealing with unusual or unexpected situations, understanding social and cultural context, and taking environmental and contextual information into account. The committee finds that the computational assists to human decision making are best when the human is thought of as a partner in solving problems and executing decision processes, where the strengths and benefits of machine and humans are treated as complementary co-systems.

In addition to these findings, the committee identified a number of promising research directions to improve the scientific basis for strong human-computer decision making:

- Data-to-decisions is an umbrella term that is not clearly defined. We need a better understanding of how cognitive functions can be supported over time and in context and an overall framework for thinking about how to design human-computer decision systems;
- The ubiquitous capability to capture, store, reproduce, move, and reuse data has led to decisions increasingly being made by networks composed of humans and machines. Yet, the exploitation of that data is often ad hoc. Research is needed to frame and systematize how we exploit that data;

- At any moment, whether a particular datum will be relevant or irrelevant into the future is task- and context-dependent, so there is an incentive to retain more, rather than less. Thus, a key challenge is to build task and context models that enable data to be filtered and processed into "useful information";
- Another challenge is developing systems that allow both humans and computers to work together in a harmonious team, rather than one supervising the other. This requires research to help individual and team exploration of (partial and incomplete) hypotheses, to enable continuous learning by the system (e.g., so the system can learn how to predict an analyst's needs and preferences); to guide continuous ingesting of data and its metadata and fusing it into the existing data; to cue decision makers to relevant, unexplored data or behavior; and to facilitate the sharing of hypotheses and derived knowledge among team members (such as by developing languages that make it easy for decision makers to state what they want the data to tell them). Creating harmonious human-computer teams would also be helped by research in comparing the different roles of humans and computers in mixed teams;
- Complex decision making often takes place in a complex environment, with multiple activities occurring simultaneously. This leads to frequent interruptions and the need to switch tasks and revise priorities. Current human-computer systems do not handle interruptions well and they need to provide more support for the resumption of interrupted activities. More research is needed on computational-interruption management techniques and algorithms, rooted in an understanding of people's cognitive and attentional capabilities; and
- More work is needed to develop a methodology for evaluating and assigning metrics for each individual piece of the collaboration and for the quality of the decisions made by the overall human-machine collaborative system.

The committee anticipates that human-computer decision-making systems will continue to advance, but this outcome is not certain. A concerted and thoughtfully guided effort will improve the chances of success.

Chapter 1

INTRODUCTION

Over the last two decades, computers have become omnipresent in daily life. Their increased power has enabled machine-learning techniques, reliable natural language processing, strong human-computer interfaces, and other capabilities that now allow computers to handle analytical tasks that were solely the domain of humans until quite recently. For example, today's navigational software helps drivers choose the shortest route to their destinations, using a combination of GPS, maps, and current traffic conditions, and it can interpret and respond to verbal commands. The step of allowing computers to actually drive a vehicle on public roads may not be far off. Similarly, computerized decision making facilitates power delivery to our homes, keeps planes in the air, and alerts our physicians about our health risks.

Along with this increasing computer power, networking technologies now make it possible for people and computers to access enormous stocks of information worldwide. Search technologies, recommender systems, database technologies, and other tools are some basic capabilities for discovering relevant information. Our ability to automate workflows and exploit distributed computing allows systems to marshal more processing power and data than most individuals or enterprises actually own and control.

This state of affairs has generated an environment that is ripe for a re-thinking of human-computer collaboration in the context of complex decision making. However, the vast amount of information that can be brought to bear does not guarantee better decisions or a more straightforward decision-making process. To build that capability, scientists, engineers, and technologists need to address a broad range of challenges as described in this report. We need a stronger foundation of knowledge in order to efficiently and reliably share tasks between humans and computers.

For example, computers are more capable than humans in finding and "digesting" huge amounts of data, and that attribute is exploited in systems such as modern electric grids, which are adjusted rapidly in response to changes in loading, and in "fly-by-wire" aviation. But the decision-making capabilities of machines are limited, in part, because their models of factors influencing decisions are limited; for instance, their models can only partially represent such human cognitive abilities as seeing the whole picture in context, including special circumstances (Hoffman et al., 2002); and being able to incorporate the implications of unexpected events and situations. Machines cannot consider the full range of decision options in part because their sensors and databases cannot provide inputs for every contingency, but also because science lacks sufficiently complete understanding to be able to foresee and include all of the variables that people may consider important. Automation can be fragile, subject to failure through mechanical problems, programming limitations, or contradictory, erroneous, or otherwise inappropriate data. Sensors measure whatever they are capable of measuring, which is seldom the actual information of most relevance to the decision maker. Human beings can be inconsistent at decision making, sometimes displaying excellence, and sometimes being prone to errors and biases. Recognition of this inconsistency has led humans to find ways to improve decision making by formalizing the process, such as through analytical methods and improved understanding of how humans and teams address decision making.

The committee believes it has been shown that technology can genuinely improve complex decision making by humans in many situations. Major computational advances over the past 2 decades have resulted in forms of computational support (data collection, data analysis, computing power, visualization, etc.) that have been readily incorporated into human decision making processes.

The specific statement of task given to the committee reads as follows:

> Conduct an analytical assessment of global research efforts in several technologies that enable humans, machines and computer systems to collaboratively digest, analyze and act on vast amounts of unstructured data in dynamic environments. This analytical assessment will include findings on
> (1) key research goals in several enabling sub-disciplines that support human-machine decision making,
> (2) main impediments to achieving technological breakthroughs,
> (3) key systems-integration challenges, and
> (4) the scope and character of international approaches to these research areas.

The sub-disciplines to be studied include, but may not be limited to: brain–computer interface, machine learning, natural language dialogue systems, sensing and perception, software agents, and cognitive and social science issues. The committee will produce a report with findings but no recommendations.

The study committee's expertise spanned the disciplines named in the Statement of Task, but its deliberations quickly revealed the difficulty in trying to bound this challenge. The following are examples of additional dimensions that are relevant to the topic under study, but which the committee decided not to cover in order to maintain focus:

- Non-technical factors that influence the success of decision making and of teams, such as emotion, social context, culture, relationships, organizational structures, authority systems, and so forth. Many such factors can lead to the failure of team decision making and are not avoided simply by improving the interactions between humans, computers, and networks. For example, great strides are being made in the development of coordination tools for distributed teams, which addresses one aspect of this. Another example is how culture affects attitudes and the politics of a region, and hence decision making. Related to that is the question of how cultural differences affect reactions to technologies, such as the degree to which new technologies are trusted and accepted. There is a good deal of emerging research on this topic.

These topics are mentioned at the end of Chapter 2's section "Overview of Decision Making," but much more could be said.
- Another aspect that could be explored more deeply is the use of feedback from decision-making teams to improve the structure and operation of decision-making processes. This is analogous to the way Facebook makes decisions about its features, interface, and interactions with people based on how its subscribers interact with one another. Big data offers the potential to improve our understanding of human networks and interactions, thus altering and enhancing the way complex decision making is managed. While the report discusses a number of ways in which big data affects (now, or potentially) human-machine coordination in complex decision making, this is an emerging area, and much more could be said.
- More generally, the report does not attempt to characterize the state of the practice of exploiting big data for decision making. A complete examination would encompass aspects such as the major approaches to learning from big data (e.g., supervised vs. semi-supervised vs. unsupervised learning) and assessing the progress and promise of various approaches (e.g., neural networks, support vector machines, Bayes graphical models). Instead of delving into these topics, the report cites and quotes from a 2013 National Academies report on the subject, *Frontiers in Massive Data Analysis*.
- The committee did not incorporate a specific discussion of human-robot collaboration and interaction because the issues involved center more around the consequences of autonomy than around the aggregation of information and coordination of team decision making. In their well-established applications, such as in factory lines, the decisions made by robotic systems are fairly prescribed and not particularly analogous to the types of interest to this study (see next chapter). However, consequences such as safety hazards[1] are persistent due to the robots' inability to sense and mitigate such hazards. Emerging applications of autonomous machines, such as self-driving vehicles and military drones, rely on more advanced decision-making capabilities[2], and thus additional concerns arise due to the possibility that actions may be taken (and properly executed) based on imperfect decision-making, perhaps with tragic consequences. These challenges cannot be properly addressed in this report.
- The committee did not delve deeply into ways to aid the cognitive work of sensemaking and computational models of attention. Some key references for these topics are introduced in the section on Human Cognition and Memory in Chapter 3 and in the section on Neuroscience in Chapter 5.

This report explores ways that people and computer systems can collaborate so that complex decisions involving large amounts of data and tight time constraints are better

---

[1] See, e.g., John Markoff and Claire Cain Miller, As robotics advances, worries of killer robots rise, *The New York Times*, June 17, 2014.

[2] See the National Research Council 2014 report, *Autonomy Research for Civil Aviation: Toward a New Era of Flight*. Washington, DC: The National Academies Press.

made. The immensity of the topic prompted the committee to give priority to outlining the context in which human-machine collaboration for decision making can profitably be discussed. This raises many research issues concerning team decision making among humans, and then similar challenges are identified when the "team" is extended to include humans and machines. In addressing these topics, the report discusses the nature of the research, achievements, and systems-integration challenges of several enabling technologies that underlie human-machine collaboration for decision making.

A 2012 workshop at the National Academies explored the topic of intelligent human-machine collaboration. It is instructive so see the range of ways in which participants at that workshop answered the question, "What Is Intelligent Human-Machine Collaboration?" The following sample of responses was quoted in the published summary of that workshop:

> "… machines and humans combining each other's strengths and filling-in for their weaknesses and empowering each other's capabilities;
> "… joint and coordinated action by people and computationally based systems, in which each have some stake in the outcome or performance of the mission;
> "… humans AND machines jointly perform tasks that they would not be able to perform on their own;
> "… integration of AI into machines;
> "… humans and machines are able to mutually adapt their behavior, intentions, and communications;
> "… cooperation that mimics interactions between two humans;
> "… naturalness of the observed human-machine interaction;
> "… neither human nor machine treats the other as a disturbance to be minimized.
> "… machines being partners, and not a tool, for humans;
> "… technology that amplifies and extends human abilities to know, perceive, and collaborate;
> "… better overall performance of the mission, independently of how it was achieved;
> "… shared responsibility, authority, goals."[3]

Overall, one can see the breadth of this topic and the absence of precise definitions and boundaries.

This report begins by examining the kinds of decisions that motivated the study. They are largely characterized by the availability of large amounts of information of varied types, which introduces a certain type of complexity. (Other types of decisions can be very complex for other reasons, such as the need to balance a range of perspectives and/or appropriately consider serious or sensitive consequences. The study that led to this report devoted less attention to such drivers of complexity.) Having laid out that context, the report discusses major human, computer, and network elements of team decision making. It then surveys the research frontiers that provide the basis for human-machine collaborative

---

[3] National Research Council. Chiang, E. N., and Wrightson, P. S., rapporteurs. 2012. *Intelligent Human-Machine Collaboration: Summary of a Workshop*, The National Academies Press: Washington, D.C. Quoted material from p. 2 (ellipses in original).

decision making, with an emphasis on building an integrated view, and offers thoughts on future directions for such research.

More specifically, Chapter Two provides the context for the question that informs this study: How might humans and computers team up to turn data into reliable (and when necessary, speedy) decisions? Here the committee looks at the three basic components of this question: the essence of decision making; the vast amount of data that have become available as the basis for complex decision making; and the nature of collaboration that is possible between humans and machines in the process of making complex decisions.

Chapters Three and Four examine, respectively, the human elements and the machine and network elements of team decision making. Chapter Three addresses several aspects of human decision making that can benefit from computer-aided systems, such as cognition, errors in judgment, and task allocation. Chapter Four focuses on the teaming of humans and computers to make decisions, and ends with a discussion on how metric classes might contribute to advancing human-machine decision making. Chapter Five looks at research areas that underlie human-machine collaboration for decision making: sensing, software agent systems, neuroscience, and human computation.

Chapter Six contains observations about where this research may be headed. Findings related to research opportunities are included in that chapter, while other findings appear throughout the report where appropriate.

In Appendix B, the report recounts committee visits to research organizations in both Singapore and Germany, but it does not assess the quality of research.; The goal of these overseas site visits was to address item (3) in the study charge, concerning "the scope and character of international approaches to these research areas."

Throughout this document, the terms and words "computational system," "computer," "machine," "information system," and "automation" are used interchangeably to make the document more readable. Given that people are experts at interpreting context, each of these words or their derivatives are also used in ways that are not interchangeable in a few places.

Chapter 2

COMPUTING AND DECISION MAKING TODAY

The study's sponsors came to the National Academies with a problem: The amount of inputs for complex decision making, and the availability of computing assistance for that process, has outpaced our ability to efficiently and effectively exploit it all. How, they asked, might humans and computers team up to turn data into reliable (and when necessary, speedy) decisions?

While the study's sponsors did not want to give details about the specific kinds of decisions they are targeting, nor to confine the committee's thinking to particular types of decisions, one can imagine that military planners today are faced with enormous amounts of information that might provide some value for critical decisions. Consider, for example, the process for deciding how to approach a destination in a hostile environment. The decision-makers may have access to tremendous amounts of heterogeneous information, though not all of it available predictably. Some information is collected over the longer term, such as knowledge about roads and bridges, inferred social networks, patterns of individuals and organizations, social schedules (market days and hours, religious services, regular meetings), the attitudes of nearby populations, and general environmental conditions. Along with that, near-term information is gathered about particular threats, weather and wind conditions, influxes or outflows of population (e.g., for special events). Aerial images, emergency calls, media reports, information traffic over social media, and "data exhaust"[1] also provide valuable information. Each of these sources has its own uncertainties, and the quality and variability of the sources may be interdependent: for instance, the attitudes of surrounding populations can change depending on what information is communicated day by day, and by the positioning of troops. Decision making for some processes, such as a multi-day approach to a new location, might unfold through a number of smaller-scale decisions; whereas decision-making in some other cases, such as whether or not to order a drone strike, is a single yes-no decision with high consequences.

Other military decision making can be even more complex. Consider, planning for a major deployment. The multi-month needs of the force must be anticipated, supply chains established, logistics planned, and so on. These demands have existed for centuries, and since at least World War II a strong foundation of analytical tools has been developed. But with today's information technology, the amount of information that can be assembled and the number of options that can be examined have grown tremendously. As an operation unfolds, it will build on reports and forecasts about weather, tide, wind, and storm conditions, movements of others on transportation routes, aerial images and other sensed data, human-generated reports from the field, media and intelligence reports, information traffic over social media, data exhaust, and so on. This broad range of information strains the capabilities of the tools and of the planners to

---

[1] Data exhaust refers to information that systems collect in the course of their work, as opposed to information that a user explicitly views or incorporates. It includes such data as time/date stamps, GPS coordinates, records of past actions by the user, and so on. A well-known example is the use of misspellings gathered during previous searches to improve the front-end interpreter used by search engines.

make good use of it all. At the same time, the relative ease with which inputs can be assembled has opened the door to compressing the decision making timeline, which further challenges the human planners.

Decision making of similar complexity occurs in many other contexts. Teams that manage the response to major disasters, such as damage from Hurricane Sandy in the United States or from the Fukushima Daiichi nuclear accident in Japan, must incorporate a very broad range of information from multiple heterogeneous sources—e.g., satellite images, local reports, scientific projections, and various communication flows—and quickly generate or update plans on multiple scales, ranging from immediate actions to staging of resources. The response to the 2013 Boston Marathon bombing is another case, one that may be more akin to some military decision making. In addition to multiple, partial information, the decision makers who managed the immediate response had to incorporate preliminary forensic evidence, crowd sourced inputs (of untested value), and other inputs, all with a great deal of time pressure. The decisions constituted a family of choices, such as where to deploy police, which areas to consider high risk for citizens and police, top-priority search areas, the best information to follow or expand, and how to conduct the search.

In all of these cases, the decision making is a team effort, with many experts evaluating information and using their analysis and judgment to create portions of the overall decision or plan. Overlain on that is a process by which team members challenge one another and jointly merge their individual insights to create a bigger picture. Ultimate decisions are made by team leaders based on this funneling of information and analysis. It is difficult for humans to make good decisions in such complex situations. It must be remembered that the ultimate goal is to make good decisions: merely finding a way to analyze and incorporate all the data is not valuable unless it also leads more reliably to good decisions.

Computational support in the form of large-scale data collection and analysis, visualization, etc. has been readily incorporated into some human decision making processes. For example, computation is in the control processes for all manner of processing plants (chemical processing, nuclear power generation and petroleum refining), infrastructure (electric grid and telecommunications), manufacturing (chip fabrication and large scale baking plants), assembly (electronics and automotive robotic assembly), transactions (credit card and banking) and the military (management of theater operations).

The rest of this chapter focuses on the three components of such complex decision-making: the essence of decision making; exploiting the vast amounts of data that have become available as the basis for complex decision making; and the nature of collaboration that is possible between humans and machines in the process of making complex decisions. The committee chose not to address whether, and if so how, autonomous systems might someday replace humans as decision makers in complex situations.

OVERVIEW OF DECISION MAKING

Decision making is integral to the human experience. Our ability to consider the implications of future actions, ponder cause and effect, and leverage our exquisite executive function capabilities sets us apart from the rest of the animal kingdom. Yet our decision making prowess is far from perfect, and some might argue that it is getting worse as we face a wave of decisions that we are ill equipped to deal with using human cognition alone.

As decision makers ponder a web of interconnections among people and automated systems, they wonder which connections matter, how disruptive a single choice will be on the overall system; how to weigh uncertainty or the potential for misunderstanding, misinterpretation, or someone else's deception; and how to analyze decision making in circumstances where there is no "right" answer. In addition, some decisions must be made against (near) time constraints. A decision not to act (or a failure to decide at all) *is* a decision in some dynamic, rapidly-changing environments. In addition to reaching a decision about a course of action, one also must make decisions about which information to consider out of the vast amounts that are available, weighing the cost of obtaining the information against its potential value. Such decisions about process can affect the quality of the ultimate decision, and they may be challenging in many of the same ways because of the multitude of options available.

The term "decision making" is itself a simplification; it refers to a process of evaluating information and reaching an actionable policy or strategy. Decision making tends to be context dependent; it often requires understanding of not only the observed or experienced situation but also of the relevant history and background.

Early theories of decision making focused upon serial processing models, where sensor processes fed perception and the several memory systems under study (working, or short-term, memory, and long-term memory) in a relatively straightforward process. Decision making itself was presumed to be a logical deduction from the information provided, and these models were often described in the language of traditional information technology and processing. Thus, the widely cited OODA-loop model originated by John Boyd has a series of primarily sequential stages: Observation, Orientation (analysis), Decision, and Action (with feedback from the stages of decision and action as well as from the environment back to the orientation stage). Although a useful paradigm for training—it was designed for situations requiring a rapid response time, such as decision making by fighter pilots, so it is necessarily simplified—it is a coarse model for studying the frontiers of decision making it oversimplifies the underlying processes. As a result, although widely referred to in operational situations and for training, it is not a common framework in the research community.

Recently the military literature has addressed the inadequacy of the OODA loop to deal with complex situations where the decision maker does not have access to a model of the underlying mechanisms between actions and outcomes (Benson and Rotkoff, 2011). For example, a "red team" approach, in which a team of experienced personnel is explicitly charged with undermining the ability of "blue" decision makers can be a valuable method for exploring a broader range of scenarios, including those that a decision-making team might deem as very low probability. A red team could identify ways in which observations might be made misleading, decisions anticipated, and actions countered, thus undercutting the applicability of an OODA-loop description of the decision-making process.

In addition, the implied sequential nature of the OODA loop—even if there is feedback between stages and perhaps multiple trips through the loop—does not fit well with real, complex decision making. In responding to a natural disaster, for example, decision making is extremely interactive, which is not modeled well with an OODA framework. And in situations for which a large amount of potentially useful information is available, it may be desirable to perform multiple versions of the observation stage—assembling several different pictures of reality—and/or to carry out multiple versions of the orientation (analysis) stage. Both of these exercises create alternatives to be assessed, possibly by following through to develop a family of potential decisions which are then evaluated before a final decision is reached.

A speaker at one of the study's early meetings suggested that human-machine-network decision making might be improved by adjusting each stage of the OODA loop to make better use of the human-machine-network "team," such as by identifying good ways of apportioning cognitive load across those three components for each of the stages. The committee believes that the OODA-loop construct is not well matched to complex decision making with large volumes of information; while the four stages are part of any decision-making process, they can be combined in multiple ways. Consequently, it developed the following finding:

Finding 1. A common representation of the decision-making process, used to train fighter pilots in rapid decision-making for air combat, calls for sequential steps to observe, update beliefs, choose an action, and take the action (the so-called OODA loop). While those steps are inherent to any careful decision making, for complex decisions the OODA loop framework does not readily reflect feedback loops between the steps and branching to consider multiple choices of action, both of which are common. The study of decision making in complex situations, and the design of automated decision support systems, requires an understanding of those complexities. Thus the OODA-loop framework may not be sufficient in these contexts.

Early decision-making models tended to assume that decision making occurred at the conscious level of processing. A more nuanced view was presented by the theorist, J. Rasmussen (1983), who divided the decision-making process of skilled operators into three categories: Skill-, Rule-, and Knowledge-based procedures. Skill-based behavior refers to those capabilities that are sensory-motor and developed after a period of training, such as riding a bike. Rule-based behavior refers to those that are based on learned rules or procedures, such as following a recipe. In this taxonomy, knowledge-based processing is the highest level of cognitive control because it includes the challenge of solving novel problems (Cummings, 2014).

Today's decision-making theories assume that much more complex cognitive processing is occurring, much of it subconscious and involving neural networks that interact as a dynamical system, with considerable iteration, feedback, and continual adjustment of parameters. For example, recent evidence about human thought implies that decisions by experts are often reached subconsciously, with reason and logic coming afterward to justify the decision (Mercier and Sperber, 2011).

Recognition-primed decision making (Klein, 2008) involves rapid pattern matching to the situation, one of the powerful properties of fast, subconscious systems. Klein's work has been of particular value in guiding decision making in complex situations—real situations, not the simplified, artificial settings studied by laboratory-based researchers.

Heuristics and rule-following present a mix of behavior at the conscious and subconscious levels of processing. At the subconscious level, researchers have identified numerous heuristics that people use to simplify and speed up decision making—effectively, pattern matching to situations previously experienced. This decision making is often referred to as fast and frugal (Gigerenzer and Goldstein, 1996). The quality of the decisions is determined by whether appropriate information is examined—driven not only by what is available, but also by the adequacy of the decision maker's implicit model and handling of biases—and by the history of prior experiences (see Mercier and Sperber, 2011; Gigerenzer, 2008; Gigerenzer and Todd, 1999).

The past decade has seen significant progress in developing technologies and methods that support human sense-making and decision-making processes in complex domains. Understanding the dynamics of a complex system or organization can help one foresee the side effects of a decision or anticipate events before they occur. Many studies have been undertaken on measuring and supporting situation awareness, especially for individual decision makers, but there are still major gaps in our understanding of how to design and evaluate technologies and methods to provide effective cognitive support for individual and team sense making (Klein et al., 2006a, b; Moore and Hoffman, 2011) and decision making (e.g., Schmorrow et al., 2012).

Traditional models of human decision making focus entirely upon mental processing—all the action takes place in the brain—but another important trend in our understanding of human behavior is to understand the role of embodiment—that the human body exists in the world, interacting with it in ways that enhance our ability to function. Norman described it as a melding of knowledge in the head and knowledge in the world, because when accomplishing some task, the environment provides much of the information required as well as providing constraints, guides, and suggested courses of action (Norman, 1988, 2013). The research field called "embodied cognition" has expanded this notion, incorporating not only the environment but also the way that the entire body is used to enhance decision making (Todd and Gigerenzer, 2007; Kirsh, 2013; Dourish, 2001).

Information systems can be designed to support the human decision maker in tasks or subtasks that are domain or situation specific. However, the quality of support afforded will necessarily depend on the skill and foresight of the software's creators. Designers of today's analytic support systems have begun to build them so that they interact in a more naturalistic way with humans. More and more systems are able to respond intelligently to queries in natural language (e.g., Apple's "Siri" and Google's "Google Now") and, as speech understanding progresses, this usage is expected to increase both in coverage and in power.

Indeed, in many of today's activities, decision making is no longer an exclusively human endeavor. In both virtual and real ways, technology has vastly extended people's range of movement, speed, and access to massive amounts of data. Consequently, the scope of complex decisions that human beings are capable of making has greatly expanded—for example, Google's technology helped to quickly map the impact of the 2010 earthquake in Haiti and then helped to develop a person-finder tool. At the same time, some of these technologies have also complicated the decision-making process. For example, social networking was responsible for many false claims just after the Boston Marathon bombing in April 2013, and subsequently, throughout the hunt for the perpetrators.[2]

In addition to meeting the challenge of supporting its intended user, systems that incorporate data analysis can encounter situations in which hostile entities intend to deceive the decision maker. When such strategic actors are present, they might play a meta-level role in determining what we are able to observe. These potential vulnerabilities must be considered when designing and using information systems as decision aids. For example, our actions, including further information gathering, can inform adversaries about our current state of knowledge.

---

[2] See, for example, "Social Media's Rush to Judgment in the Boston Bombings," http://www.npr.org/blogs/alltechconsidered/2013/04/23/178556269/Social-Medias-Rush-To-Judgment-In-The-Boston-Bombings. Last accessed March 19, 2014.

A decision-making context and process can be characterized along dimensions such as the following:
- Whether a single decision is to be made, a sequential cascade of decisions made in discrete or continuous fashion, or some complex construct of multiple-related decisions, possibly made by numerous people in concert or solo;
- The pace of decisions: real time, seconds, minutes, days, years, or decades;
- Any clear trigger that characterizes the point at which a decision is forced; this might be the observation of a provocative action, the impending loss of a desirable alternative for action, or the closing of a narrow window in which an intervention can be effective;
- The degree of confidence that must be reached in order to justify a decision; if there is a trigger, a low weight of evidence might suffice, but in other cases the inevitable uncertainties in information and models must be characterized and factored in;
- The number of decision makers, their relation to one another, their diversity, and the responsibility and authority of each;
- Resources available to the decision makers (limited, adequate, rich);
- Scalability: if the relevant, available data that can be processed during the decision-making process is large, and possibly dynamic;
- Cultural differences;
- Rules of engagement that enable or constrain options; and
- Quality and availability of relevant data
    - Stale, inadequate data
    - Data from different sources: people, computers, and sensors that may be of different kinds and varying performance
    - Complexity of structure and formats (audio, video, image, electromagnetic, handwritten)
    - Data location: collocated, geographically distributed across a network
    - Levels of certainty associated with each data source.

The list above characterizes many aspects of the human decision-making process, and each dimension will influence an information system that is designed to support decision making. Any or all of these dimensions might be considered when developing such an information system.

Many other factors have crucial effects on decisionmaking, such as emotions, social context, relationships, organizational structures, authority systems, and so forth. And the way individuals work in networks can have strong impacts. Ignoring these factors can lead to failures of team decision making, and an understanding of these factors must inform the design and incorporation of technologies. Currently, tools that assist with team coordination are making great advances. For example, Facebook is able to learn how its subscribers interact with one another and make decisions about the site's features and interfaces based on that information. Analogous technology that uses big data to understand human networks and interactions is also affecting other important decisions such as where to distribute malaria nets in Africa, where to send emergency teams in a disaster, how to advertise a political candidate, and how to induce people to contribute to charity. Culture should also be considered, because it affects team-members' attitudes and unspoken assumptions, such as how they feel about privacy, trust, sharing, and so on. There is a good deal of emerging research on this topic.

BIG DATA

We live in an era of "big data."[3] Today, big data are everywhere, and datasets are growing in size, noise, and complexity—experiments, observations, simulations, images, video, text, networks: Science and business are generating terabytes of data and greater, and the scale of social media data can extend into the exascale range. More and more, these data are considered potential sources of knowledge, requiring increasingly sophisticated analysis techniques to uncover their relational and semantic underpinnings. Indeed, it could be argued that much of the drive toward big data has been bottom up: Let's collect more data and then analyze it and hopefully derive knowledge (which at times may only be correlations rather than causal knowledge).

Arguably, we currently stand at the beginning of a decades-long trend toward increasingly evidence-based, data-informed decision making across all walks of life. This trend is powered by the confluence of several technical and societal trends that are projected to accelerate over the coming years: the exploding volume and variety of data, the accelerating use of the Internet to share these data and to support team decision making, and the widespread adoption of personal mobile devices that give individuals nearly continuous opportunities to communicate, to collect data about themselves and their surroundings, and to access online computer assistance.

Analyses of massive datasets have already led to breakthroughs in fields as diverse as genomics, astronomy, health care, urban planning, and marketing.[4] For example, credit card companies now make better decisions about which credit card transactions are likely to involve fraud by scrutinizing millions of historical credit card transactions to automatically discover the subtle marks that distinguish fraudulent from acceptable charges. Local governments use historical and real-time data feeds to improve decisions about traffic control and about where and when to allocate foot police to keep the peace. Individuals now use mobile devices to capture continuous data about the number of steps they take every day, their weight, and other personal health data in an effort to understand and improve their own health. We are also beginning to witness new ways in which groups of networked individuals can work together to make better decisions: Social network sites invite visitors to play games that design new proteins (Foldit) or use their differing expertise to answer one another's questions (e.g., Yahoo! Answers, Quora).[5]

Big data poses tremendous opportunities—the promise of having much improved understanding of the many elements of relevance to our questions and choices—but also great challenges, because creating that "understanding" requires much more than simply finding the information. The process of inferring true knowledge from it is non-trivial. The sheer volume of the data requires computing just to prepare and filter the data for human interpretation. But that may not be enough, because the filtered output can still be enormous, and current capabilities

---

[3] The term "big data" is an umbrella term that refers not only to the vast amounts of data that computers now make available but also to "a transformation in how society processes information," what Kenneth Neil Cukier and Viktor Mayer-Schoenberger call the "datafication [of] many aspects of the world that have never been quantified before." *Foreign Affairs*, May–June 2013. http://www.foreignaffairs.com/articles/139104/kenneth-neil-cukier-and-viktor-mayer-schoenberger/the-rise-of-big-data. Last accessed March 24, 2014.
[4] See, for example, *The Fourth Paradigm* (2009).
[5] See https://fold.it/portal/; https://www.quora.com/; https://answers.yahoo.com/.

cannot filter out all noise, such as errors and spurious patterns. Humans excel at some of these steps: for example, a typical Internet search can yield thousands or millions of "hits", some very much related to the query, and some very far afield. The fact that appropriate results are often at the top of the list is an amazing accomplishment, but it is still necessary for a user—an analyst— to assess the top N hits to determine which are most promising. Humans are remarkably good and fast at this, thus exceeding the capabilities of computers, although even then, humans can be fooled by erroneous information, superficial associations, manipulation of search engines, and other artifacts of the data or the algorithms that filter it. And for many cases, it is not feasible to simply dump search results onto an analyst's screen because there may be too many relevant results for a human to check. Even if feasible, the timeliness of decision making will then be limited by the speed of a human analyst.

Finding 2. Increasingly the data used to support computer-assisted decisions are drawn from heterogeneous sources (e.g. unstructured text, images, simulation outputs). Current techniques for filtering and aggregating these disparate data types into a well-characterized input for decision making are limited, which therefore limits the quality of the decisions.

Thus, the response to big data appears to be "big computing." Computers are undisputedly better than humans at keeping track of myriad details, filtering and organizing massive amounts of data.[6] Algorithms give us needed information at our fingertips nearly instantaneously. Yet it is still often the case today that the human has to adapt to the machine, rather than the other way around. It is important to understand and quantify the unique capabilities of the human and the information system to allow both to function optimally.

It is also critical to recognize that exploiting large bodies of data is not necessarily better than traditional approaches. Smaller amounts of data, including data drawn via a process of sampling from large stores or streams of data, may provide the most important inputs to decision making.

As discussed in detail in the 2013 National Research Council report *Frontiers in Massive Data Analysis*, there are still substantial challenges for massive data. These range from the more "familiar" domains of storage, indexing, and querying to "the ambitious goal of *inference*" (italics in the original) needed for decision making, which the report defines as

. . . the problem of turning data into knowledge, where knowledge often is expressed in terms of entities that are not present in the data per se but are

---

[6] That said, human vision and cognition still far exceed machine-based vision and cognition in many areas. A 2008 report from the National Academies (*Emerging Cognitive Neuroscience and Related Technologies*) observed "The global scientific computing community is approaching an era in which high-end computing will, in principle, be sufficient in capacity and computational power to model the human brain. However, there does not yet exist either an adequate and detailed understanding of how such modeling can be done, nor a complete model of how the brain interacts with complex regulatory and monitoring systems throughout the body. These and other difficulties make it highly unlikely that in the next two decades anyone could build a neurophysiologically plausible model of the whole brain and its array of specialized and general-purpose higher cognitive functions."

> present in models that one uses to interpret the data. Statistical rigor is necessary to justify the inferential leap from data to knowledge, and many difficulties arise in attempting to bring statistical principles to bear on massive data.
>
> (National Research Council, 2013)

Among these hurdles are sampling bias, provenance, and control of error rates. All statistical methods rely on assumptions about how the data were gathered and sampled; however, massive datasets are often constructed from many subcollections of data, each of which was amassed using a different sampling scheme for a different purpose. The analyst may have little control or insight into this collection. Further, the "data" may not be the original observations, but may be the product of previous inferential procedures, and, without care, subsequent analyses can amplify noise.

Finally, the temptation with massive data is to multiply the number of hypotheses explored, and this can lead to substantial issues with "false discovery."

Finding 3. While improved information availability can improve the quality of decision making, more information alone is not sufficient. This is particularly evident in complex scenarios where the goals of different team members are not completely aligned and delays make it difficult to attribute effects to actions.

Although existing statistical tools can address these issues, much work remains to be done in developing and applying them to massive data. In particular, there is still a gap: the middleware that would enable statistical tools to interact with distributed systems. The Committee on the Analysis of Massive Data (2013) identified several key research areas:

- Data representation, including characterizations of the raw data and transformations that are often applied to data, particularly transformations that attempt to reduce the representational complexity of the data;
- Computational complexity issues and how the understanding of such issues supports characterization of the computational resources needed and of trade-offs among resources;
- Statistical model building in the massive data setting, including data cleansing and validation;
- Sampling, both as part of the data-gathering process and as a key methodology for data reduction; and
- Methods for including people in the data-analysis loop.[7]

Much of the current report focuses on the final research area listed above.

---

[7] See *Frontiers in Massive Data Analysis* (2013), 4-5.

FROM TOOLS TO TEAMMATES[8]

In the early days of computing, machines were slow, they lacked today's software power, and they communicated poorly with humans. Such computers could be programmed to perform well-understood, limited, and often repetitive tasks. They could display almost real-time radar returns, hold and represent text for an author, and list inventory. In these situations, the automation executes minor, even incidental, tasks that support human decision making. The results provided are useful, but the computers are not centrally involved in determining how the decision process is orchestrated over time. Humans have tended to delegate discrete tasks to computation, such as searching for information in a data base, mining large volumes of data, depicting information in visual form that is more amenable to human understanding, and monitoring some behavior (such as streams of credit card transactions or surveillance camera recordings).

Advances in computing capabilities over recent decades now make it reasonable to consider how to integrally incorporate automation into complex decision-making systems. This progress has enabled human beings and computers to assemble into networks composed of geographically dispersed members. As computing devices have gained increasing abilities to intelligently interpret information and to act over long periods of time with diminished human supervision, their ability to act as teammates rather than simply be tools has increased. Although the distinction between tool and teammate is not a sharp one, the difference in experience working with a device that is a teammate rather than simply a tool is powerful. For instance, consider two systems that might help a person in writing a paper. The tool-system allows the person to easily reach Google and search for citations. The teammate-system goes farther and provides some functions akin to what a colleague could bring to the partnership. For example, based on a few "hints" (authors, keywords) provided by the user, the teammate-system would then operate autonomously and in parallel with the user to perform additional searches to find candidate papers and citations. The system may have used machine learning to generate additional inferences (perhaps from a history of the user's own searches, or from a textual analysis of the user's past writing) about the user's unstated intent for the automated searching. Or it may have generated a family of such information based on previous examinations of the user's colleagues. When the user is ready, the teammate-system presents the results of its searches, and perhaps some analyses; when the user has selected (in this case) references to include in the paper being drafted, the system can do all formatting required so that text is ready to drop into place.[9]

Categorizing an automated element as a tool or a teammate does not carry great importance, except to recognize that the relationship between humans and computers is changing. The capabilities described in the last paragraph may look primitive before too many years have elapsed. The pertinent challenge is to determine strategies for improving human-machine systems that engage in complex decision making or, stated another way, how to

---

[8] This phrase refers to the article "From Tools to Teammates: Joint Activity in Human-Agent-Robot Teams," Jeffrey M. Bradshaw et al. (2009).
[9] See, for example, Tamara Babaian, Barbara J. Grosz, and Stuart M. Shieber, "A Writer's Collaborative Assistant," *Proceedings of the Intelligent User Interfaces Conference*, (San Francisco, CA), 2002. ACM Press. Available at http://dash.harvard.edu/handle/1/2252600. Last accessed April 8, 2014.

structure decision making in the face of enormous amounts of information and computers with very strong, but specialized, capabilities.

Cognitive scientists have examined a wide range of decision-making activities involving mixed teams composed of people and machines (e.g., Hollnagel and Woods, 2005). Computer scientists in the fields of artificial intelligence and multiagent systems have formalized collaborative behavior, developed specifications for system design, built computer "agent" systems with teamwork capabilities, and developed "collaborative interface systems" (e.g., Grant et al., 2005; Gal et al., 2010). This work has taken a perspective very different from the older descriptions of human-computer systems in which the various skills and weaknesses of people were compiled and used to attempt to determine how best to partition task components between person and machine (e.g., Fitts, 1951; Parasuraman et al., 2000). It has led to a variety of frameworks for describing possible relationships between humans and automation in the carrying out of complex tasks (e.g., Miller, 2012).

New capabilities in automation and ubiquitous connectivity are making it increasingly feasible—and feasible in novel ways—to connect humans with a larger and broader set of automation types, including vehicles and other assets. As noted in Miller (2012). "Control" can now exist along a spectrum of multiple operators, perhaps at multiple levels of an organization, and it can be shared in various ways among them.

In the future, each human or machine participant might:

- Proffer information or observations or suggestions to team members that advance some aspect of the shared objectives;
- Proffer critiques of the team's problem-solving strategies;
- Possess "self-awareness" when approaching overload and recruit help in such a situation;
- Monitor teammates' problem-solving process and execution, and then anticipate the information needs of others; give and accept feedback; identify gaps in approach; and cover for another's execution failure;
- Explain how a result was reached; and
- Adjust activities over time to account for changing needs of the team and its members; adapt as the decision scenario unfolds.

This point of view that sees human-machine decision making as a collaboration echoes the 2012 Defense Science Board report *The Role of Autonomy in DoD Systems*:

> The Task Force reviewed many of the DoD-funded studies on "levels of autonomy" and concluded that they are not particularly helpful to the autonomy design process. These studies attempt to aid the development process by defining taxonomies and grouping functions needed for generalized scenarios. They are counter-productive because they focus too much attention on the computer rather than on the collaboration between the computer and its operator/supervisor to achieve the desired capabilities and effects. Further, these taxonomies imply that there are discrete levels of intelligence for autonomous systems, and that classes of vehicle systems can be designed to operate at a specific level for the entire mission.[10]

---

[10] Department of Defense Science Board, *Task Force Report: The Role of Autonomy in DoD Systems*. Washington, DC, 2012, p. 3.

Viewing the system as a team offers a framework for exploring avenues toward a more effective overall process or processes, which in turn will dictate the design of the automated components as well as how the participants interact.

The technological advances outlined above have enriched or promise to enrich the relationships and potential between humans and automation as well as the quality of decisions they produce. To fully exploit this situation, engineers can use a growing number of design techniques for building and structuring human-machine decision-making teams. The committee analyzed multiple aspects of the machine-human relationship. Members discussed opportunities to achieve better decision-making processes as well as problems that arise when the design does not sufficiently honor the strengths and weaknesses of the two types of participants, as will be discussed in the following chapters.

Chapter 3

HUMAN ELEMENTS OF TEAM DECISION MAKING

While human-machine collaboration differs substantially from human (only) teamwork, it helps first to understand how humans work together in teams in order to understand the expectations that humans have for teamwork situations. This chapter focuses on several elements that affect human teams, such as decision analysis, trust, memory, and accounting for human error; it ends with a brief discussion on task allocation.

DECISION ANALYSIS

Humans rely on their fast intuitive decision making capabilities in many situations but, when decisions are complex and the stakes are high, a slower, more deliberative process based on decision theory and decision analysis is worth using instead. Such a process does not try to predict or mimic intuitive human decision making but instead decomposes complex problems into their component parts, so as to take actions based on normative engineering principles.[1] It provides more consistency between the actions taken in similar situations and more transparency in the reasoning and judgments used to choose those actions. This transparency also allows machines to use these same component parts to make decisions and to support human decision makers.

    Underlying the decision analysis approach is a Bayesian view of the world, where the decision maker's beliefs about uncertain distinctions and quantities are represented with probabilities, continuously updated to reflect the decision maker's observations. The decision maker's initial beliefs are represented explicitly and can therefore be informed by expert judgment. However, those beliefs can become insignificant when there is sufficient relevant data.

    The two other components needed to make decisions are alternative choices and preferences over prospective outcomes. The alternative choices are represented by a set of available actions in a given situation, and the preferences by a utility value for each outcome. At any given point in time, the decision maker should take the action that provides the greatest utility, taking into account the probabilities and utilities of the possible outcomes that can result from the action. Therefore, we can distinguish between the quality of a decision, based on the reasoning that went into it, and the quality of the outcome, which was still uncertain when the decision was made. All of this is set within a decision frame, the underlying context that captures the appropriate uncertain distinctions and alternative choices.

    When facing or anticipating a decision, the best action is often to gather more information. The decision maker must weigh the cost of the information in time, money, and other resources against the benefit arising from the ability to change and improve the choice depending on what will be observed. If the decision maker would make the same choice

---

[1] E.g., Hammond, J.S., Keeney, R.L. and Raiffa, H. *Smart Choices: A Practical Guide to Making Better Decisions*. 1999. Harvard Business School Press.

regardless of what information will be revealed, it would not be worth gathering.

The quality of the decision can depend critically on access to all of the relevant information available. It is important to develop methods for recognizing which data sources are useful for particular decisions and which are not. When multiple information sources are available, the decision maker can use a model to account for any relationships among them. In situations involving data with systematic errors or potential deception, the decision maker can interpret the data by a similar modeling process, and thereby learn indirectly about the distinctions of interest.

Many parameter judgments are needed to represent the decision maker's beliefs and preferences. Performing sensitivity analysis, seeing how the choices and their values change when these parameters are perturbed, can identify which parts of the model are less robust, where additional information gathering would be most valuable and improve the quality of the decisions.

Graphical models, such as Bayesian belief networks and influence diagrams, have been valuable tools for building, communicating, learning, and analyzing models among decision makers, experts, analysts, and machines.[2] They also help identify which sources of information might be relevant for particular decisions. There have been many promising and fielded applications using these methods, with applications as diverse as Space Shuttle engine monitoring,[3] genetic analysis,[4] and breast cancer diagnosis.[5] However, there are still many outstanding challenges associated with decision analysis, such as difficulties determining a utility function or assessing outcome probabilities, and our limited ability to model human behavior.

---

[2] See, e.g., Koller, D, and Friedman, N, *Probabilistic Graphical Models: Principles and Techniques,* 2009. Cambridge, MA: MIT Press; Miller, A.C., et al., *Development of Automated Aids for Decision Analysis*. 1976, Stanford Research Institute, Menlo Park, CA; Pearl, Judea, Probabilistic reasoning in intelligent systems: Networks of plausible inference. 1988, San Mateo, CA : Morgan Kaufmann Publishers; Pearl, Judea, *Causality: Models, Reasoning, and Inference*. 2nd Edition, 2009, New York: Cambridge University Press; and Shachter, R.D., Evaluating influence diagrams. *Operations Research*, 1986.34(November-December): 871-882.

[3] Horvitz, E, Ruokanga, C, and Srinivas, S. A Decision-Theoretic Approach to the Display of Information for Time-Critical Decisions: The Vista Project, In *Proceedings of SOAR-92*, NASA/Johnson Space Center, Houston, TX, 1992.

[4] Fishelson, M, and Geiger, D, Exact genetic linkage computations for general pedigrees, *Bioinformatics*. 2002. 18, p. s189-s198.

[5] Beck, A.H., Sangoi, A.R., Leung, S., Marinelli, R.J., Nielsen, T.O., va de Vijver, M.J., West, R.B., va de Rijn, M., and Koller, D., Systematic analysis of breast cancer morphology uncovers stromal features associated with survival, *Science Translational Medicine*. 2011, 3(108):108-113.

HUMAN TEAMWORK

Teamwork has become the strategy of choice when organizations are confronted with complex and difficult tasks.[6] The study of human team performance has produced a considerable body of knowledge, and recent discoveries have important consequences for human-automation collaboration.[7] Technology has had a strong impact on the structure and operation of teams. In particular, coordination tools (e.g., networked systems, bots) are advancing greatly.

In human teams, work is assigned according to a number of considerations, including particular individual competencies, quantity and quality of appropriate resources, time constraints, and availability. Thus, in a human team, someone with enhanced mathematical or statistical expertise would normally be assigned to tasks requiring this kind of knowledge and skill, but during the course of the activity, if some other aspect requires more aid, these people would shift to help. Similarly, if the mathematical or statistical workload rose too high, less qualified workers would assist, ideally doing lower-level assignments that match their abilities. The important point is that team members typically concentrate upon their areas of expertise, but the division of labor remains flexible.

There are benefits to rotating assignments among team members so that every team member experiences the others' activities. This practice provides training that allows substitutions (albeit, not always perfect ones) when the situation demands. It also provides each team member with a deeper understanding of the requirements and difficulties of colleagues' tasks. This familiarity enhances the communication and interaction among team members even when they are doing their primary tasks (Nikolaidis and Shah, 2013; Hollan, Hutchins, and Kirsh, 2000; Hutchins, 1995). Indeed, great teams tend to distinguish themselves by how well they manage soft interdependencies, i.e., emergent opportunities to offer and receive help that are not part of one's explicit job duties (Johnson et al., 2014a).[8]

This rotation of assignments may or may not include the team leader. In some cases, the team leader's understanding of external context might not be shared in any depth by the team's member, and the leader may not have the technical skills to serve on the team. But if those conditions do not hold, and the work schedule can withstand some disruption, rotations involving the team leader can help the team better understand how its work feeds into the bigger context. Plus, the experience can broaden the team's thinking because a temporary change in leadership can introduce new thoughts about priorities, processes, and relationships.

When automated systems are available, team benefits may accrue if the human team members occasionally take on the tasks of the nonhuman agents. For example, in flying an airplane, the automation might be turned on or off, depending on the overall workload. By deliberately not using the automation, other team members could learn what that component does and, moreover, remain practiced at performing that task in case the automated system fails. Team members may also attain a better understanding of what the automated system *cannot* do—for example, an airplane pilot might be able to visually spot potential sources of turbulence ahead and take early action, whereas the automated system would rely on different sensors and perhaps be delayed. In some situations, though, such as robot-assisted search in inhospitable

---

[6] See Salas et al., 2008; Cooke et. al., 2012; Wildman et al, 2013.
[7] See McKendrick et al., 2013; van Wissen et. al., 2012; Cuevas et al., 2007.
[8] We thank an anonymous reviewer for the thoughts presented in this paragraph.

environments, human substitution might not be possible at all. In others, the person and machine could collaboratively guide the behavior through teleoperation. It would even be better if the automation did not have to be either on or off, but rather could be biased and guided. Humans can guide and teach the automation and, in turn, the automation can guide and teach humans. Ideally, the human team members will learn about the limitations of the automated system, including any points of failure, so as to develop a realistic sense of how much trust they can have in the automated assistance.

Recent research by Tausczik, et al. (2013), and of Woolley, et. al. (2010) works to elucidate the effectiveness of groups based on characterizations of their composition and of the functioning of ideal groups for problem solving.

COMMUNICATION: ESSENTIAL AND CHALLENGING

Communication is critical, whether the teams are purely human or a mix of humans and machines. Quite often, when difficulties arise, they can be traced to insufficient or inappropriate communication, although a mismatch of skills does play a role (Bradshaw et al., 2013). Three major communication challenges are: (1) what information to convey to other teammates, (2) which teammates to communicate with about this (new) information, and (3) when to communicate. These questions need to be addressed for both human and machine members of a team, and when a communication traverses a human/computer interface, additional care is necessary to ensure that the receiver and sender share the same implicit assumptions about the information and that the receiver knows how to interpret the information.

In a fully cooperative team, all members communicate as needed. Of particular importance is communicating about the status of tasks they are doing or their own performance as limits are reached. Thus, when one set of team members starts to become overloaded, they are apt to signal this by stating that they might need some help, alerting other team members to look over their activities and to step in when required. Even when a member is not overloaded, they may be reaching the edge of their comfort zone, in terms of performing tasks with which they are less capable or for which the available information is inadequate. In those cases, adding another team member with different skills, or splitting the workload, may not address the problem. The most important mitigation might be for other team members to recognize that some additional uncertainty may be creeping into the overall process, so they can take steps such as slowing down, adding redundancy, or relying more on other members.

Many failures of automated systems come from a lack of communication of their activities. We see this in the crash of Asiana Airlines Flight 214 at the San Francisco airport on July 6, 2013. The airport's vertical guidance service for instrument landings was not operative, so manual control of the glideslope was required. The lack of complete communication and awareness of the states of the airplane and of the automated equipment, coupled with the pilots' understanding of these states, have turned out to be a factor in this incident.[9]

---

[9] See *The New York Times,* June 25, 2014. P. A-11. "Flight crew missed multiple cues before San Francisco crash, board says."

TRUST

While all teamwork requires the establishment of appropriate levels of trust, collaboration between humans and machines raises the issue of human trust in the inanimate teammate.[10] If people on the team are to rely and act on contributions and recommendations of automation, they will do so only if they have confidence that the teammate will make a positive contribution, plus some sense of how much, and in what ways, they can trust the automation. Such trust must be earned.

Operators' lack of trust in automation—and the resulting possible disuse of data that it presents—limit the potential that technology offers. However, operators' inappropriate excessive trust and the resulting automation misuse could lead to complacency and the failure to intervene when the technology fails or degrades (Cummings, Pina and Crandall), or has not been programmed for the appropriate circumstances (Parasuraman and Riley, 1997; Lee and Moray, 1994; Hoffman et al, 2013). A nuanced understanding is needed: for example, a complex decision might build on information from different searches (each with its own blind spots or ambiguities), different databases (with differing levels of quality), statistical inferences (with complex uncertainties), and simulations, which are only imperfect models of reality. Somehow, the team—and the ultimate decision-maker—must aggregate these inputs, taking into consideration the degree of confidence that each can contribute to the decision.

Several elements affect the development of an appropriate level of trust, i.e., trust calibration (Hoffman et al., 2012, 2013). The machine should perform reliably and predictably, measured in timeliness and accuracy of response. It should contribute information that is valuable to the decision-making process and deliver this information to the appropriate people or machine agents. Further, it is important that the people relying on automation understand the basis for the machine's decision or recommended action. To do so, computer-based participants require algorithms and heuristics that are able to reason about the information's importance and significance at a given time to a given individual, and are able to receive and display information about the basis for its recommended action. In addition, if a computer can teach or assist a human trainee so that the novice can perform at a higher level, the machine will have gained some trust. One important component of trust is observability: In the absence of appropriate observability (communication), people (or machines) may be unable to calibrate their trust appropriately—undertrusting competent human/machine behavior or overtrusting human/machine behavior—because the signals that would allow them to perceive problems are insufficiently salient or absent altogether.[11]

Consider two human-machine systems, each of which aims to provide perimeter monitoring around a building complex. Assume that imaging devices are mounted so that, in combination, they maintain a persistent view of the surrounding space. The simple system just records and displays images. Guards watch the images in one or more control rooms. These

---

[10] Automation's trust of humans bears consideration, but it was not discussed to any extent by the committee.

[11] E.g., Hoffman, R. R., J. D. Lee, D. D. Woods, N. Shadbolt, J. Miller, and J.M. Bradshaw. The dynamics of trust in cyberdomains. *IEEE Intelligent Systems* (2009, Nov/Dec), pp. 5-11; Hoffman, R. R., Matthew Johnson, J.M. Bradshaw, and Al Underbrink. Trust in Automation. *IEEE Intelligent Systems*, January/February 2013, 28(1) 84-88.

humans are responsible for making all decisions about whether to act, when to act, and what action to take.

The second system includes teamwork between the machines and humans, which requires much more sophistication in the automation and, more importantly, a different design philosophy. In this imagined system, the automation would include image analysis, detection, and recognition algorithms or heuristics. It would alert the humans when it sees unusual changes. It might identify and characterize objects or creatures and communicate those observations. It might be programmed to take action on its own cognizance—to sound alarms, for example, or turn on lights in the area of suspicious activity.

Concurrently, the human operators would observe the same scene (with appropriate displays of the information gleaned by the sensors and perhaps some machine-generated suggestions or inference). They would work with the system and determine what trust they place in the automated teammates. They too might identify and characterize objects or creatures and communicate those observations. They might take action on their own cognizance—to sound alarms, for example, or turn on lights in the area of suspicious activity. They might question the automation's conclusions and/or direct it to attend more carefully to particular aspects. The human operators might thus enhance and supplement automated actions, helping to continuously train the machines (if so designed), and/or contravene them. Perhaps they would come to trust that the system will always alert them to any suspicious activity. The number of humans on watch might be reduced, and they might discontinue their scrutiny of image displays because they know that the automation will perform reliable detection. But they might find that the analytic software often mischaracterizes entities, mistaking dogs for small unmanned ground vehicles or people, or failing to distinguish multiple trespassers from one. The humans on this team might have confidence that the automation can detect an intrusion, but not that it can identify the intruder. In this situation, the humans might restrict the authority of the automated teammate to nondestructive action. This scenario also points toward issues of assessment—for example, if the machine could accurately report the degree of confidence with which it has identified the interloper, the humans might give it more rights to act if those measures exceeded some threshold. This last item points toward the desirability of research into methods that evaluate the confidence level of a potential decision maker, and some such techniques might apply to humans as well as machines.[12]

In short, the team members would mutually observe, analyze, and decide upon the course of action, each using the perceptual skills and knowledge that they are best suited for. Furthermore, the level of human or automated involvement could be modified over time, depending on evolving levels of trust. A key observation is that in all of the scenarios the human is supervising the machine, although the level of supervision may diminish as the trust and understanding grow more nuanced.

The military as well as field intelligence and law enforcement teams operate with clearly specified rules of engagement. Decisions about what authority to delegate to an automated element are weighty. The committee considered the extreme end of the military context—whether any circumstance would warrant conferral upon a machine the ability to "pull a trigger" with a human "outside the loop." The response to that issue depends heavily upon the degree of human trust in automation that has accumulated through observation of the machine's behavior

---

[12] See, for example, how IBM's Watson applies confidence levels to its answers on the television show *Jeopardy* on February 16, 2011. Available at https://www.youtube.com/watch?v=YLR1byL0U8M.

in a variety of situations. The committee assumes that for the foreseeable future, these kinds of decisions will remain with humans. However, it also recognizes that decisions that fall short of "pulling the trigger" can also be dangerous—a machine could bias some of the contributing information in a way that leads a human to a decision they would not make if they had better ground truth—and is mindful that decision making that depends on human-machine teams can introduce risks.

Finding 4. Computer assists to human decision making will "come of age" when some of the computational elements are not simply assistive, but perform at a level that they are trusted as "near-peer" teammates in an integrated human-computer system. One of the key challenges of this integration will be the development of new techniques for test and evaluation that build trust between the human partner and the computational elements.

HUMAN COGNITION AND MEMORY

In the past decade, our understanding of human cognition has undergone major change. There is greater understanding of the interplay between the relatively slow, linear mental processes of consciousness and the rapid subconscious mechanisms that involve parallel processing. Progress on computational models of attention is providing new tools to design and test whether a system taps into these fast, parallel processes or overloads deliberative forms of cognition.[13] Balancing fast parallel processes with executive processes that test for relevance is a critical part of the cognitive work of sensemaking, which is a critical aspect of analytics and for melding the capabilities of humans and machines. Sensemaking is especially important to the ability to critique or test results from machine partners.[14]

In addition, our understanding of human memory systems is undergoing rapid change. Human memory is a powerful pattern matcher, capable of finding information from prior experiences that are analogous to the current experience. This gives the human unparalleled ability to form new connections and to use related experiences successfully in new applications. However, this same powerful ability is also subject to numerous biases. For one thing, human memory is reconstructive. That is, what is recalled is not a precise compilation of prior experience, but rather a reconstruction based upon current conditions and expectations. This can cause difficulties that lead to error when the reconstruction does not in fact reflect an authentic statement of that prior experience. Worse, the reconstruction then is irreversibly retained along with the original experience. Each memory retrieval therefore impacts what is retained in memory (Oudiette et al., 2013). A danger in memory retrieval is that once a person finds what appears to be a match, they can become locked into that as a solution and therefore are unable to give fair assessment to other alternative possibilities.

A second aspect of human memory is that there are numerous subsystems that retain different kinds of information (e.g., semantic, declarative, episodic) and different temporal durations (e.g., working, or short-term memory; long-term memory). Working memory is

---

[13] For example, see Itti, Laurent; Geraint Rees; and John K. Tsotsos, *Neurobiology of Attention*, Academic Press, 2005.

[14] We thank an anonymous reviewer for contributing important points to this paragraph.

particularly susceptible to interference. It only holds a relatively small amount of information at any moment and is highly susceptible to interference by other events, such as intervening tasks.

The best cooperative systems will couple the powerful capabilities of human memory for (a) rapid pattern matching and (b) analogical, metaphorical extrapolation of past events to new situations, with the accuracy and completeness of the memories of computational systems.

Systems can enhance working memory by keeping an active display of all current information (properly grouped and displayed to make it easy to access relevant items without further increasing computational load). By ensuring that all items needed for the current decision are readily available working memory can be enhanced. If the person is multitasking, having each separate task display its relevant working memory set in a different, but well-marked, location has the potential to reduce the interference caused by multitasking and make it easier and faster for a person to recover situation awareness when switching among tasks. Note that the graphical display is critical: It must be designed with good, psychologically-derived, design principles to ensure minimal computational workload.

Pattern-matching memory can be enhanced by providing aids to recover specific stored information relevant to the person's decision process. If a person thinks "this is just like situation Z" the ability for a computer to retrieve information about situation Z would minimize the distortion that might accompany a person's memory reconstruction.

Similarly, the system might also provide other situations that it has determined relevant (much as a book-recommending system points out that the book being looked at is similar to specific other books). This would also lessen the risk of a person prematurely focusing on a similar (but different) early event. Note that computer systems are only partially successful at detecting true relevance, being subject to both misses and false alarms, but if the presentations are done well, the inaccuracies do no harm and might even help in encouraging the human operators to critically assess the suggestions rather than simply accept them blindly.

Even though we do not know the underlying architecture of human processing and decision making, there is considerable helpful observational evidence about the resulting behavior, to help us see which kinds of situations lend themselves to decisions being made rapidly and efficiently, situations that lead to poor decisions, and the strengths, weaknesses, and biases of the process.

A highly over-simplified model that helps put much of the behavioral observations in perspective simply asserts that conscious processes are relatively slow, serial, and limited in the amount of information that can be maintained in an active state, especially in relation to time-stressed decision making. Novel information is particularly difficult to maintain, and conscious attention is severely limited. Conscious processing has very limited computational resources available to it so much so that only a few different threads can be tracked at the same time. (Some theorists would argue that "few" is one, or perhaps two, if the two are related to one another.)

Subconscious processes are fast, efficient, and parallel, with multiple processes operating at the same time (in different cortical areas of the brain). They tend to do energy minimization, which is a kind of pattern-matching process. Well-learned, familiar patterns that are consistent with the information available are attracted quickly to stable configurations (attractors, in the language of dynamical systems). As a result, people can be very efficient when dealing with known situations: Give them a little bit of information and they settle into a stable solution. This is the basis for many psychological phenomena, where people, objects, and even complex situations can be identified extremely rapidly, far before there is sufficient information to provide a reliable estimate.

But the rapid capture by familiar patterns is also a source of bias that can lead to erroneous decisions. The more overlap there is between the current situation and previous ones, the more likely the decision maker is to be trapped by an attractor that represents an earlier situation. Once there, it is very difficult to get out even when discrepant data arrive. Remember, there is often a superabundance of data, much of which is irrelevant: Sifting out the relevant from the irrelevant is difficult until some sort of working hypothesis is formed, but once the hypothesis exists (often because a stable configuration has been identified), anchoring can occur and discrepant data may be filtered out as irrelevant. Here is where the joint operation of humans and machines can have an advantage: When one system gets stuck in a local energy minimum, the other system can gently nudge it out of that state. Work on computational models of attention gives designers a mechanism to tap into these states and modulate the outcome. Research reveals, for example, that it is possible to track, measure and model human attention in real-time with relevant stimuli.[15] This work is confirmed by human psychophysiological studies,[16] and these models can be implemented in systems to help provide the "nudge" that a human observer might need to dislodge from prior expectations. As models are both improved by neuroscience studies and in turn used to improve performance of humans, we expect this area to be widely implemented in visual detection tasks. As the systems become engaged semantically, in addition to capturing visual features, they will approach the collaborative systems that we have been envisioning for complex tasks. These models should be consciously designed into the networked systems. Otherwise, the well-studied frailties of human judgment and decision making (e.g., Tversky and Kahneman, 1974), especially in the face of uncertain information, will continue to limit the quality of decision making.

But the rapid capture by familiar patterns is also a source of bias that can lead to erroneous decisions. The more overlap there is between the current situation and previous ones the more likely the decision maker is to be trapped by an attractor that represents an earlier situation. Once there, it is very difficult to get out even when discrepant data arrive. Remember, there is often a superabundance of data, much of which is irrelevant: Sifting out the relevant from the irrelevant is difficult until some sort of working hypothesis is formed, but once the hypothesis exists (often because a stable configuration has been identified), anchoring can occur and discrepant data may be filtered out as irrelevant. Here is where the joint operation of humans and machines can have an advantage: When one system gets stuck in a local energy minimum, the other system can gently nudge it out of that state. These models should be consciously designed into network systems. Otherwise, the well-studied frailties of human judgment and decision making (e.g., Tversky and Kahneman, 1974), especially in the face of uncertain information, will continue to limit the quality of decision making.

---

[15] See Itti, Li and P. F. Baldi, A principled approach to detecting surprising events in video. In: *Proc. IEEE Conference on Computer Vision and Pattern Recognition* (CVPR), pp. 631-637, June 2005.

[16] So for example, Itti, Li and C. Koch, Computational modelling of visual attention, *Nature Reviews Neuroscience*, 2(3):194-203, March 2001.

ERRORS IN HUMAN JUDGMENT AND DATA

Teams make errors, which arise from a range of sources, including social dynamics, time and resource constraints, inappropriate communication, and erroneous and/or incomplete data and/or thinking. In addition to the multitude of judgment errors that can arise from flawed data and faulty thinking or weak information processing on the part of an individual, other systemic challenges crop up—for example, the ability to discover errors.

Researchers have divided human errors into two broad classes: slips and mistakes (Norman, 1988, 2013; Reason, 1990; Woods and Branlat, 2010). A slip occurs when an intended action is not performed. A mistake occurs when the intention is wrong. Both types of errors transpire in the context of human decision making.

A slip is relatively easy to detect, because a comparison of the intended action with the actual one reveals a discrepancy. Mistakes are difficult to detect, because the actual actions match the intended ones, but the intention is wrong. People's actions are consistent with their misguided intent and there is nothing to signal that it is the intention that is wrong. Because mistakes are difficult to detect, they are by far the more worrisome error.

Mistakes fall into three major classes: rule based, knowledge based, and memory lapse. In a rule-based mistake, the person has appropriately diagnosed the situation, but then decided upon an erroneous course of action by following the wrong rule. In a knowledge-based mistake, the problem is misdiagnosed because of erroneous or incomplete knowledge. Memory-lapse mistakes take place when forgetting occurs at the stages of goals, plans, and evaluation.

The decision theory perspective is a helpful way to think about how to deal with inevitable errors. In that context, the best action is a function of the current situation, the actions available now, the estimated probabilities of possible outcomes of the actions, and the estimated utilities of each outcome. Mistakes can be made at each point: not knowing what the current situation is; not recognizing all possible actions; missing some possible outcomes from an action (or their likelihood), and not knowing how good or bad a certain outcome will be. This complements the categorization of errors into a rule-based, knowledge-based, and memory-lapse taxonomy.[17]

Even when a mistake is the result of a faulty diagnosis of the situation, it can be surprisingly difficult to discern. One might expect that the actions would turn out to be ineffective, so the discrepancy would be noticed, leading to a reexamination of the diagnosis. But misdiagnoses are not random. Usually they rely on considerable knowledge and logic. The misdiagnosis is often logical and it might help eliminate observed symptoms, at least at first. As a result, the initial actions tend to be relevant and helpful. This situation makes the challenge of discovery even more difficult and can postpone it for hours or days. Mistakes caused by memory lapses are even more difficult to detect: The absence of something that should have been done is always more difficult to detect than the presence of something that should not have been done.

A major difficulty in discovering mistakes occurs because people tend to lock themselves into the solution, blinding themselves to alternative explanations. The mistaken hypothesis or intention is usually rational and, more often than not, appropriate. If it is not appropriate, many of the observed symptoms are still consistent with the mistaken interpretation. Moreover, inconsistent observations are easily explained away. Note that complex situations involve huge quantities of observations, many of which are irrelevant. Distinguishing signal from noise,

---

[17] We thank an anonymous reviewer for the thoughts presented in this paragraph.

however, is often possible only after the nature of the signal has been determined. A working hypothesis can help decision makers sift noise from signal, but if the wrong hypothesis is being entertained, inappropriate sifting can occur. Improved methods to identify the sources of variability (or noise) that affect data quality and contribute to decision "correctness" might be useful.

Individuals and teams can also err by explaining away problems when they should not. Seldom does a major accident occur without a prior string of failures such as equipment malfunctions, unusual events, or a series of apparently unrelated breakdowns and errors. No single step has appeared serious, but by overlooking these precursors, a major disaster can brew. In many of these cases, the people involved noted and discounted each item, finding a logical explanation for the otherwise deviant observation.

To some extent, this practice is necessary. Many potentially suspicious things that teams could pay attention to would turn out to be false alarms or irrelevant minor events. At the other extreme, teams could ignore every apparent anomaly and rationally explain each one.

Because of their ability to store large bodies of precursor information and sift through it to find patterns, computers might be suited to assisting humans at identifying potentially problematic patterns. Machines could help focus attention on particular events that have proved problematic in a past case or which deviate too far from their normal range. Automation might be particularly helpful when large quantities of data are emerging within a short time frame. Improvements in normality modeling, which should help identify exceptional behavior in any particular context, could help humans identify activities of interest.

Another common error is that events can seem logical in hindsight. The contrast in our understanding before and after an event can be dramatic. The psychologist Baruch Fischhoff (1975) has studied explanations given in hindsight, where events seem obvious and predictable after the fact but had not been predicted beforehand.[18] When Fischhoff presented people with a number of situations and asked them to forecast what would happen, they were correct only randomly. He then introduced the same situations along with the actual outcomes to another group of people, asking them to state how likely each outcome was. In that situation, the actual outcome appeared plausible and likely, and other outcomes were ranked as unlikely.

Foresight is difficult. During a complex situation, clear clues do not necessarily emerge. Many things are happening at once; workload, emotions, and stress levels are high. Many events will turn out to be irrelevant, while things that appear irrelevant will turn out to be important. Accident investigators, working with hindsight, focus on the pertinent information, but when the events were unfolding, the operators could not distinguish one from the other (see Woods and Branlat, 2010). Decision-makers who are sorting through large amounts of information and complex interplays of options can be faced with the same challenge.

---

[18] A modern treatment of this issue is provided by Duncan Watts in his book *Everything is Obvious: Once you Know the Answer*. New York: Crown Business (2011). Available at www.everything is obvious.com.

TASK ALLOCATION

Historically, engineers have tended to assign operations to either humans or machines depending on their capabilities (Christoffersen and Woods, 2004), or they have automated as much as possible, leaving leftover tasks to humans. In both scenarios, people are expected to take action when the automation ceases or fails. Furthermore, they often must enter data into computer systems in ways that are easiest for the machine to understand and interpret. As a result, precise, unambiguous, and numerical inputs dominate, which often need to be delivered in a repetitive manner. Humans must be attentive for long periods, mostly monitoring events that require no attention, yet ready to respond immediately and effectively to rare emergencies. Finally, people are asked to absorb and synthesize data that are not necessarily presented in a way that is optimally suited for the human brain.

This approach has long been viewed as problematic.[19] It requires the more versatile and capable teammate, the human, to rescue the more limited machine, often with no advance notice. The human frequently must act rapidly, with little situation awareness. People are not good at responding quickly when they have been out of the loop. Moreover, we are not skilled at precision, repetition, or continued vigilance. Rather, people are versatile, adaptive, and attentive to a wide variety of events. Thus, instead of being matched to human strengths, the machine requirements are often matched to human weaknesses. People's ability to cope under most circumstances masks the system's fragility; as a result, failures are blamed on human error instead of inappropriate overall design. This is at odds with a basic tenet of high-reliability organizations: that systems and processes should be engineered to reduce the risk of errors—which are inevitable—and to be robust when errors do occur.

People and machines possess distinctive capabilities and frailties that are actually often complementary. That feature thus provides an opportunity for enhancing system performance by leveraging that complementary. Data-presentation choices, for example, might rely on cutting-edge knowledge about how the brain works, and software might organize otherwise overwhelming datasets. This process would include considerations about different ways to allocate tasks among humans and machines, and it would take into account how duties might change over time, depending on circumstances.

Finding 5. Humans and computation have different strengths in what they accomplish and there are several aspects of human decision making that can benefit from computer-aided systems, such as cognition, recognition of errors in judgment and task allocation. Similarly, there are several aspects of computer processing that can benefit from human guidance, such as prioritization, dealing with unusual or unexpected situations, understanding social and cultural context, and taking environmental and contextual information into account. The committee finds that the computational assists to human decision making are best when the human is thought of as a partner in solving problems and executing decision processes, where the strengths and benefits of machine and humans are treated as complementary co-systems.

In this view, the participants—humans and machines—might, at some point, share the load more evenly and take the lead on duties that naturally fit their respective capabilities. Cross-

---

[19] The critique goes back at least far as Paul Fitts (1951).

training combined with awareness about work assignments could allow transitions in tasks to occur naturally and gracefully among team members. A human who is overloaded or incapacitated (perhaps from injury or sleep deprivation) might ask a machine to take over some lower-level work. An overloaded or incapacitated machine (perhaps due to some system failure) might alert people that it is reaching its limits. Humans and machines might hand control and authority back and forth.[20]

With this perspective, one aims to understand the potential for joint collaboration between computational systems and people and to determine the design criteria and strategies needed to ensure that this is a real collaboration, where each contributes their best strengths and where communication among team members, including between people and machines, are always in the appropriate language and interactive form. A key challenge is to make sure design honors the need to address human characteristics, as opposed to today's interaction, which typically is dictated by the needs of the machine. That is, to design so that systems adjust or adapt to people rather than presuming people will adjust to them (which often is stressful or does not work).

---

[20] See discussion of Frank Flemisch's work in Chapter 4, Flexible Human-Machine Interaction, p. 44.

Chapter 4

MACHINE AND NETWORK ELEMENTS OF TEAM DECISION MAKING

The previous chapter looked at several of the human elements that bear on decision making. This chapter examines several technological areas that play a role in collaborative human-machine decision making and appear to have promise for enabling advances in human-machine collaboration. The chapter ends with a brief discussion of metrics that can help assess human-machine collaboration for decision making.

MIXED HUMAN-COMPUTER TEAMS

While there are extensive studies of human teamwork in varied contexts,[1] further studies of the characteristics of successful decision-aiding automation in the context of hybrid human-automation teams are warranted.[2]

Recent work on the foundations of team cognition helps to fill the need for further empirical studies of team performance that can elicit key attributes for the design of decision-aiding automation. The dominant perspective in psychology on team cognition is shared cognition, which assumes as its basic construct that some form of mental model is shared among individual team members.[3] This has recently been critiqued as inadequate to explain decision-making performance in large, spatially distributed teams because in such settings, individuals can hold only partial views of the situation. Thus, for spatially distributed decision making, coordination across collections of partial knowledge is key. In fact, it has been argued that team cognition is grounded in the interactions among team members rather than in their shared knowledge structures (Cooke et al., 2013). This appears to be a promising direction.

Many approaches to designing team-like cooperation between humans and machines have been proposed, including adaptive supervisory control, adaptive automation, dynamic task

---

[1] See, for example, Cummings et al., 2010; McKendrick et al., 2013; Salas et al., 2008; Dekker and Woods, 2002; de Winter and Dodou, 2014; Pritchett, Kim, and Feigh, 2014; Jarrasse, Sanguineti, and Burdet, 2014; Woods and Branlat, 2010; Cuevas et al., 2007.

[2] The Human Factors and Ergonomics Society has dedicated its fifth annual contest in 2014 for the best paper on "human factors/ergonomics research that pertains to effective and satisfying interaction between humans and automation" (http://www.hfes.org/web/pubpages/hfprize.html).

[3] See, for example, S. Fiore and J. Schooler. Process mapping and shared cognition: Teamwork and the development of shared problem models. In *Team Cognition: Understanding the Factors that Drive Process and Performance*, E. Salas and S. Fiore, eds., American Psychological Association, 2004. See, also E. Entin and D. Serfaty. Adaptive team coordination. *Human Factors*, 41, 1999. S. Fiore, E. Salas, and J. Cannon-Bowers. Group dynamics and shared mental model development. In *How people evaluate others in organizations: Person perception and interpersonal judgment in industrial/organizational psychology*, M. London, ed. Lawrence Erlbaum Associates, 2001. R. Hoeft, J. Kochan, and F. Jentsch. Automated team members in the cockpit: Myth or reality. In *Advances in Human Performance and Cognitive Engineering Research*, A. Schulz and L. Parker, eds.. Elsevier Science, 2006.

allocation, adjustable autonomy and mixed-initiative interaction. To underpin novel design requirements, researchers in cognitive systems and artificial intelligence have identified a number of general requirements for team-like interactions among humans and automation (e.g., Christoffersen and Woods, 2004; Klein et al., 2004; Johnson, 2014b; Bradshaw et al., 2013). Of particular relevance to this report are the concepts of (a) mutual predictability of teammates, (b) establishment and maintenance of common ground, and (c) ability to redirect and adapt to one another. The discussion on coordination in joint activity follows Klein et al. (2004).

Mutual Predictability (Klein et al., 2004): To be a team player, an intelligent agent—like a human—must be reasonably predictable and reasonably able to predict others' actions (Sycara and Lewis, 2004). It should act neither capriciously nor unobservably, and it should be able to observe and correctly predict its teammates' future behavior. One risk of making automation more adaptable is that it might make its behavior less predictable. To make actions sufficiently predictable, targets, states, capacities, intentions, changes, and upcoming actions should be obvious to the people and automation components that supervise and coordinate with them. Note that this requirement runs counter to the advice sometimes given to automation developers to create systems that are barely noticed.

Common Ground (Klein et al., 2004): Perhaps the most important basis for interpredictability is common ground (Clark and Brennan, 1991), which refers to the pertinent mutual knowledge, mutual beliefs, and mutual assumptions that support interdependent actions in a joint activity. Common ground refers to the process of communicating, testing, updating, tailoring, and repairing mutual understandings and permits people to use abbreviated forms of communication, such as head-nods (or an automation analogy) and still be reasonably confident that potentially ambiguous messages and signals will be understood. It also includes what parties know about each other prior to engagement—for example, the others' background and training, habits, and ways of working.

Directability and Mutual Adaptation (Klein et al., 2004): Directability refers to deliberate attempts to modify the actions of the other partners as conditions and priorities change. For example, as part of maintaining common ground during coordinated activity, and relying on mental models of each other, team members must expend effort to appreciate what each other needs to notice, within the context of the task and the current situation. It pushes the limits of technology to get the automation to communicate even close to fluently as if it were part of a well-coordinated human team working in an open, visible environment. The automation will have to signal when it is having trouble and when it is taking extreme action or moving toward the extreme end of its range of authority. Such capabilities will require interesting relational judgments about agent activities: How does an agent tell when another team member is having trouble performing a function but has not yet failed? How and when does automation effectively reveal or communicate that it is moving toward its limit of capability? (Christoffersen and Woods, 2004).

The major computational models of collaboration developed by researchers in multiagent systems[4] all treat teams as more than a collection of individuals and collaborative activities as

---

[4] See, for example, Levesque, Cohen, and Nunes, 1990; Grosz and Kraus, 1996; Kinny et al., 1992.

more than the summation of individual activities, and to varying extents have specific computational mechanisms to capture the above-mentioned requirements. The formal specifications in these models include commitments by team members to the team activity and each other's actions, requirements for communication to ensure team members are in sync and aware of the state of each other's activities, and requirements or mechanisms for reasoning about the skills of potential team members and allocating (and possibly reallocating) tasks among team members.

Other relevant work includes efforts to provide people with new tools and platforms that enable them to solve problems jointly and to tap into larger crowds of people and their intellect. Many relevant studies have been done in the Computer-Supported Collaborative Work (CSCW) community, including work to develop tools that allow multiple problem solvers to participate in problem solving. (See, e.g., H. Zhang, et al. Human Computation Tasks with Global Constraints, CHI 2012, Austin, TX, May 2012. http://dl.acm.org/citation.cfm?id=2207708.)

Other efforts and examples with importance for the topics discussed include work to develop more flexible representations of the degree of autonomy that machines have in hybrid human-computer systems. An example may be found in Scerri, et al. (Paul Scerri, et al. Towards Adjustable Autonomy for the Real World (2003). *Journal of Artificial Intelligence Research* 1 (2003) 2-50. http://www.cs.cmu.edu/~pscerri/papers/JAIR-AA.pdf). [5]

SYSTEM BRITTLENESS AND RESILIENT SYSTEMS

The previous discussion focused on the cognitive expectations that humans have when working in human or mixed human-computer teams. In addition, humans expect their counterparts to be able to work—that is, to function properly—and to be flexible. Yet automated systems have tended to be brittle. They are rigid and, when overloaded, they break down suddenly, often without warning (e.g., see Smith, McCoy, and Layton, 1997; Bass, 2013); alternatively, they do not completely stop working, but they lack the flexibility to catch up with ongoing activities. Brittleness poses multiple problems. For example, in aviation, automated systems fail when the demands upon them become too high—ironically, when they are needed the most.

Human performance, in contrast, tends to degrade gradually. It slowly deteriorates and maintains partial effectiveness.

Brittleness undermines a desired feature of collaborative work: the ability of members to adapt to teammates' changing capacities or behavior. If teammates know what others are doing and when they might be reaching their cognitive or system limits, they might anticipate when assistance is needed. Toward this end, enhanced self-awareness and knowledge by the automated systems could help combat brittleness and its negative effects in decision making.

People often are blamed for problems that arise from the brittleness of the systems they operate. Furthermore, routine and reliability are often emphasized and promoted among human team members—yet flexibility is often a hallmark of successful troubleshooting.

Potential approaches for addressing these challenges come through multiple avenues, including the development of "resilient systems" (e.g., Hollnagel, Woods, and Leveson, 2006)

---

[5] We thank an anonymous reviewer for the thoughts in this paragraph and the one that precedes it.

through so-called resilience engineering. Typically, an adverse event triggers investigations into what went wrong. Fewer efforts, however, tend to probe what goes right most of the time (under normal conditions) or after a positive outcome to surprise circumstances. As stated in a recent document from the National Academies, "resilience engineering focuses on the story of the accident that never happened."[6] Information that grows out of such explorations might reveal adaptive interactions or practices that "routinely produce safe and reliable performances in the presence of hazards and opportunities for failure" (ibid.). Successes as well as failures offer constructive lessons.

Resilience engineering places value on a system's ability to monitor and recognize variable and/or unforeseen events and behavior, respond, and gain knowledge from the experience. The power of this strategy stems from the observation that unexpected conditions, in the context of complex decision making, are normal and can be expected. The ability to foresee challenges and adjust accordingly increases performance quality. Unpredictability is an inherent part of any complex system and task.

Many of the powerful advances today in computational vision, language processing and translation, and reasoning rely upon statistical and sub-symbolic techniques, such as neural networks, Bayesian networks, and other machine-learning approaches instead of techniques based on deterministic logic. Because they depend on statistics and probability rather than rigid rules, these systems are frequently less brittle than systems that are purely rule- or logic-based. Another source of flexibility for some of the newer algorithms comes from incorporating self-learning instead of relying on hand-crafted rules. For instance, they can read reports and update themselves rather than relying on a static set of input data.

Although such systems can be extremely effective, they lack deep understanding of the domain to which they are applied; they can make inferences, but inferences have a non-zero chance of being wrong. People bring a variety of contextual information to bear on interpretation of data, deriving meaning that extends far beyond the raw data. Computer systems remain limited in their ability to tie individual pieces of information together and connect them with prior experience. Fundamental research breakthroughs in various subfields of artificial intelligence (including natural-language processing, automated reasoning, and probabilistic inference) are needed to increase computers' abilities to reason effectively with contextual information. For instance, such sophisticated systems as Watson and Siri interpret each single utterance in isolation. Some of the funniest errors Watson made during its Jeopardy appearance occurred when it did not bring the context into account.[7]

Several commercial and academic tools are available for automatic speech recognition (ASR), all employing some variant of statistical supervised learning. However, the performance of most systems is still relatively poor in non-laboratory environments, especially when the

---

[6] See *Ideas to Innovation: Stimulating Collaborations in the Application of Resilience Engineering to Healthcare*. Meeting Summary. 2013. Government-University-Industry Research Roundtable, The National Academies. Available at http://sites.nationalacademies.org/PGA/uidp/PGA_055253.

[7] Other promising results are starting to materialize as well. In 2012, researchers discovered that computers can identify cat faces, even when they are not directed to do so. After looking at millions of YouTube thumbnail frames, the 1000-machine network figured out—on its own—that something about cat faces is important. They accomplished this without human assistance or prelabeling of the images, based solely on patterns detected in the data. This capability mimicked, to some degree, humans' expertise at recognizing patterns that matter to us. Available at http://www.wired.com/wiredscience/2012/06/google-x-neural-network/. Last accessed March 19, 2014.

language that the dialogue participants are using is not restricted. For example, Google Voice search services have an error rate of 17 percent; Carnegie Mellon University's Sphinx system shows similar accuracy in laboratory settings but much worse in field settings (e.g., 68 percent for the "Let's Go Public" project [Raux et al., 2005a]).[8] Improved performance can be gained by using additional inputs, such as facial gestures.

Another element of natural language processing is sentence-level processing. The input to this component is a transcription produced by the ASR. The main purpose of sentence-level processing in dialogue systems is often to extract dialogue acts, which convey the action that the persons performed in its action of speaking.[9] These dialogue acts provide higher level "building blocks." Recent work also attempts to identify the emotional attitude of the human interlocutor (Forbes-Riley and Litman, 2011).[10] Current approaches to extract dialogue acts include using a context-free grammar of dialogue acts, and inferring from that the current dialogue act. More advanced methods use Hidden Markov Models (HMMs), where the states are the dialogue acts and the text detected by the ASR is the observations. The HMM is then used to return the mostly likely dialogue act sequence. Other statistical machine learning methods have also been proposed, using keywords as features.

Scientists are approaching the communication goal in numerous ways. Some are attempting to create computers whose architecture mimics that of the nervous system. If successful, such "neuromorphic" computers might rely on as-yet-undiscovered knowledge about how individual neurons and the circuits they compose enable spontaneous learning, adaptability, and multisensory integration—and how the brain achieves its renowned plasticity. Mimicking some degree of that plasticity might one day help engineers build robust automation that can rewire itself, as the brain does, if a portion degrades or fails.[11]

Future systems could integrate the approaches mentioned above, combining large datasets, computational power, and statistical and subsymbolic processing with the deeper understanding provided by appropriate sets of concepts, representations of domain-specific knowledge, and symbolic reasoning. The resulting machines might well contribute more fully to decision making. The new field of "deep learning" may produce advances along these lines.

DATA ANALYTICS

Data analytics is the loosely defined term for the set of capabilities that enables the winnowing and analysis of massive amounts of data and its presentation in a form that is interpretable by (usually) a human. It has become a key enabler in the path from data to decision. An important part of the final step—representing the information in a format that is readily and reliably interpretable—is often abetted by "visual analytics," which is considered here to be part of data analytics.

---

[8] Antoine Raux, Brian Langner, Dan Bohus, Alan W Black, and Maxine Eskenazi. Let's go public! Taking a spoken dialog system to the real world. In *Proc. of Interspeech* 2005.

[9] Stolcke, A. et al. . Dialogue act modeling for automatic tagging and recognition of conversational speech. *Computational linguistics*, 26(3):339–373, 2000.

[10] Kate Forbes-Riley and Diane Litman. When does disengagement correlate with learning in spoken dialog computer tutoring? In *Artificial Intelligence in Education*, pages 81–89. Springer, 2011.

[11] According to the 2008 National Academies study, *Emerging Cognitive Neuroscience and Related Technologies,* achieving the full vision of these goals with significant depth is still decades away.

Traditionally, data analytics focuses on using descriptive and predictive models created with statistics, operations research, and more recently, machine-learning techniques to gain insights from data. The insights are typically in the form of correlations and patterns such as association rules and groupings, discovered by posing open-ended queries, or optimal values based on some mathematical models, computed with predefined objectives. With the advent of big data, a current focus in analytics research is to address the unprecedented volume of data. Various computational algorithms and architectures (cloud, Hadoop, etc.) designed to accommodate ultralarge data volumes have emerged and gained commercial successes. But in addition to this, traditional methods of analysis must be adjusted to be efficient at large scales, or replaced by different algorithms that can scale to terabytes and beyond. Analytical methods for big data must be developed with a clear understanding of the reliability of the inferences being made because it is, if anything, easier to spot patterns and correlations when one has massive data, and some or many of these could be spurious (false positives).

Because the majority of today's data are unstructured, another key focus of data analytics is information extraction—extracting useful information and features from raw data into structured and machine-readable formats suitable for analysis. The raw data can be in structured format—for example, spatial and temporal information in the form of GPS data for vehicles, or location information of mobile phone users. It can be in semistructured or unstructured text format, such as machine logs or tweets and blogs on social media. It can even be in multimedia formats such as images and videos from surveillance cameras. In the age of big data, automated information extraction technologies must be able to process large, complex, and dynamic datasets, and analyze them together with structured data stored in traditional relational databases, often in real time. It is also important to be able to handle both human-generated and machine-generated data. Much of the current research on information extraction and data-analysis methodologies focuses on data generated by humans, such as through social media. However, as more machines begin to communicate with other machines, the fastest growing and most pervasive segments of big data will be those generated by machines for machines, through websites, applications, servers, networks, and mobile devices.

A key issue that arises in such a setting is that the data will be accumulating not just in unprecedented volume but also with ferocious velocities, thereby making their storage infeasible. As such, data analysis will have to be performed dynamically, as the data stream through the processor, often in real time. This poses a fundamental algorithmic challenge, as conventional data-mining and machine-learning approaches often assume the availability of a large set of static data. Current research in data-stream processing, event detection, and online machine learning seeks to address these issues.

In addition, the data might not only be changing continuously, but they could also be sparse, scattered, and noisy. One approach to addressing this problem is to integrate the data with additional information; for example, incorporating domain information (e.g., meta-data annotations) or combining it with additional data sources to fill some of the gaps. In traditional, small-scale data analysis, humans had the luxury of examining raw data for keystroke errors, duplications, or obvious outliers, and then cleaning up the data set before analysis. Humans are good at such functions, whereas machines are not. However, with even moderately sized data sets, and certainly with massive data, this sort of manual inspection is not feasible, so algorithms are being devised to emulate such human capabilities so as to handle this pre-processing. Data that are generated with the purpose to deceive could also be embedded in the source. It is therefore important to develop intelligent analytics techniques that are able to detect deception and misinformation within accurate real-world data. Researchers working on the development of human-machine decision making systems in such a context need access to data that are very heterogeneous and streaming in order to create appropriate methods; small-scale, controllable data sources are often qualitatively different.

The physical world itself is fast becoming a type of information system: Networked sensors are being embedded in devices ranging from mobile phones, smart energy meters, and cars to personal health monitoring devices and industrial machines that can sense, create, and communicate data about the state of the physical world. As most sensor data are monitoring some aspects of the physical world, "cyber-physical-aware" analytics algorithms that can leverage physical constraints (e.g., temporal, spatial) are useful for addressing some of the analytics challenges, and this has not been typical in past information technologies.

Data mining and machine learning discover historical patterns, associations, and relationships hidden in the data, but the interpretation of the discovered patterns to extract knowledge for decision making is done primarily by the human decision maker. As data-mining algorithms are enhanced by automated reasoning about the statistical relations discovered, intelligent decisions can be made with deep knowledge of risks, options, and consequences. Not all of this information can be derived from the data by the machines themselves. Humans, machines, and networks need to be intimately involved in the decision-making process, interactively and collaboratively.

DISTRIBUTED NETWORKS

In networked environments, decision-making processes are increasingly supported by technology. Orchestrating collaboration among humans and automation in scenarios that involve large numbers of participants and highly interconnected networks of people and machines brings challenges that do not apply to smaller teams. In particular, the scale shift in complexity, brought about by the many interdependencies across processes and activities, changes responses to key questions about what it means to be "in control."

In networked decision making, the acts of gathering data as well as data analysis and comprehension can occur over a distributed network with many humans and automated agents adding data to the system, often nearly simultaneously. Furthermore, the disparate subteams might gather the data in different ways or it might exist in different modalities at different locations; funneling and transforming this collection into a single, uniform collection poses significant challenges.

As discussed above, a key limiting factor in most human-machine interactions is communication among people and machines. Machine-design strategies often expect people to be precise and unambiguous in the issuance of commands and information (although people's skills in this area are weak), with limited information back to the people and, even then, often in forms understandable only by the technical elite. Even in relatively simple settings, studies of human performance illustrate how communication can break down between human and automation due to factors such as attention being misdirected or misfocused or goal conflicts being missed or misprioritized (Cuevas et al., 2007). Environments in which humans "control" a coupled collection of automated subsystems place increasing emphasis on complex cognitive functions such as goal monitoring, which enables shifts of goal priorities, and management of a complicated set of constraints.

Team cognition is a challenge for developers of networked human-automation systems. Shared understanding allows management of uncertainties that machines may have about humans' goals and focus of attention, as well as uncertainty that humans have about automation's plans and status. Regardless of the machine's role, creating machine understanding of human intent and making the machine's results intelligible to a human are problems to be addressed by any human-automation system. Conversely, finding ways to increase human confidence in a machine's activities, with an appropriate degree of caution, is increasingly important as computers are doing more of the predecisional work. In time-sensitive settings or where the amount of incoming data is large, humans may not be able to work through the details of what the machine has done.

In complex, networked scenarios, the imperative for establishing and supporting team cognition results in a technological need for computer-based support that can promote collaborative processes and tasks. This need is further exacerbated and complicated by the fact that the machines translate data from the real world through sensors and computers that often must process or delay the raw data. Such issues are the primary reason that human decision makers are needed, particularly in networked environments, to resolve uncertainties that result.

Finally, transitions in authority and control in cooperative systems become crucial as authority and autonomy relationships shift. Roles adjust in line with the changing demands of situations and capabilities of the team members. As systems become multilayered, these facets become harder to identify and manage. New polycentric control architectures are being developed to dynamically manage and adapt these relationships across diverse but interdependent roles, organizations, processes, and activities (Woods and Branlat, 2010).

FLEXIBLE HUMAN-MACHINE INTERACTION

To illustrate by analogy some attributes of a collaborative human-machine activity that incorporates features of shared cognition, Flemisch et al. (2003) consider horseback riding, where the horse is an analogue of a powerful, intelligent automaton. In normal situations, the rider directs the horse at a high level, but the horse takes over the details of movement, including local path planning, navigation over or around obstacles, and so on. In cases of perceived danger, the horse alerts the rider (Norman, 2007).

Flemisch and colleagues (2003) have shown how this analogy can be applied to a person's control of an automobile. Experienced horseback riders signal the horse about the degree of autonomy to be permitted. When in "tight-rein" mode, the rider exerts considerable control, even directing individual foot movements. In "loose-rein" mode, the horse is in charge, allowing the rider to relax, perhaps even to fall asleep, while the horse traverses a known trail or an easy one. These two modes are signaled by the tightness of the reins; in an automobile, similar options can be exercised by the degree of control the human exerts over the steering wheel or joystick.

A similar idea occurs in the design of the Segway, where the rider controls the vehicle speed and direction, but if the Segway determines the speed to be unsafe, it pushes back the control lever, causing the driver to lean backwards, which reduces the vehicle speed. Flemisch and associates use a similar scheme for their automobile, so if the vehicle is going too fast or approaching another car or an obstacle, the wheel-controlling device pushes back at the driver, thus signaling the difficulty and also taking control. (The driver can force the vehicle to do the action anyway, just as a horseback rider can force a horse to do an action that it resists.)

In the horse-rider situation, members of the duo do not perform equivalent roles, but both contribute to the goal. Crucial information—although not every new piece of data that each member is gathering—flows from one to the other. Decision authority passes back and forth, yet choices about some aspects of the task remain firmly assigned to either the animal or the human. Together, the horse and rider arrive at their goal faster, more safely, and more accurately than if either one had tried to make the journey alone.

The committee found this work was quite innovative, and the interplay between a horse and rider is richer and more fluid than what can currently be attained between humans and computers. For that latter reason, the metaphor may be useful in pointing to possible extensions of human-computer interplay.

Other studies of shared control between a robot and a human performing interactive motor tasks illustrate that although there is considerable interest in design for such interactions, little work so far has achieved a deep understanding of the physical interaction issues or implemented even simple collaborative behaviors (Jarrasse, Sanguineti, and Burdet, 2014).

METRICS

With the growth in research, development, and operational deployment of complex, networked systems, a need is emerging to judge whether a particular technology is adding value above and beyond a legacy system. It is often difficult to compare competing systems, because standardized performance metrics for the system or its operator or operators either do not exist or are flawed. In principle, one might want to know how much the technology or information system enhances human reasoning and understanding, how well and how rapidly it aids decision making, and how successful the decisions are.[12]

Many evaluation programs gather large sets of metrics, which often include traditional human factors such as reaction time, error rates, and so forth; such metrics, however, fail to capture the effectiveness of the human-system interaction and do not diagnose the cause of problems they expose. To gauge system effectiveness, vague and context-dependent mission performance characteristics, such as situation awareness and time to mission completion, are often collected. Although these attributes are important, it is not clear how they can equitably be compared across networked systems that involve different human-system interactions. An alternative strategy, in which massive amounts of data are collected without a clear evaluation focus at the time, might provide the raw material for standardized comparisons, but such a shotgun approach is expensive in terms of time and money.

Recent work has explored the development of metric classes for human interaction with automated systems. Much of the following discussion follows Cummings, Pina, and Donmez (2008). A metric class is defined as the set of metrics that quantify a certain aspect or component of a system. The rationale for defining metric classes stems from the assumption that particular metrics are mission specific, but metric classes might apply across different missions. Other efforts have probed robot-effectiveness metrics, human-robot interaction metrics, and

---

[12] Note that this section is dealing with metrics about the performance of human-machine teams. It is not meant to address metrics for gauging the quality of decisions.

single human–multiple robot metric classes.[13] Metric selection is inherently linked to the practitioner's objectives and depends on the context and resources available, which reflects the inherent cost-benefit nature of such endeavors. Detailed discussions about selecting appropriate metrics through consideration of criteria such as experimental constraints, construct validity, statistical efficiency, and measurement-technique efficiency can be found elsewhere (Donmez and Cummings, 2009; Cummings and Donmez, 2013).

When humans and automation are working in complex, networked arrangements, it is essential to evaluate not only the performance of individual humans and machines but also the complex interactions among team members. Furthermore, one would like to know how these metrics relate to the overall system. Such a task poses numerous challenges, especially in situations where team members and the jobs they are executing are distributed in space and time.

Researchers (Pina, Donmez, and Cummings, 2008) have proposed five metrics classes with which to assess individual components as well as holistic systems:

- Mission Effectiveness – For example, key mission-performance parameters relating to the whole human-automation system.
- Autonomous Platform Behavior Efficiency – For example, usability, adequacy, autonomy, learnability, errors, user satisfaction, automation speed, accuracy and reliability, neglect time.
- Human Behavior Efficiency – Operators perform multiple tasks such as monitoring autonomous platform health and status, identifying critical exogenous events, and communicating with others as needed. How humans sequence and prioritize these multiple tasks provides valuable insights into system design effectiveness.
    - Information processing efficiency (e.g., decision making)
    - b. Attention allocation efficiency (e.g., scan patterns, prioritization)
- Human Behavior Precursors—The underlying cognitive processes that lead to specific operator behavior, as compared with the human behavior metric class that captures explicit behavior.
    - Cognitive precursors (e.g., situation awareness, mental workload, emotional state)
    - Physiological precursors (e.g., physical comfort, fatigue)
- Collaboration Metrics—That is, team-level metrics.
    - Human-automation collaboration
    - Automation-automation collaboration
    - Human-human collaboration

The final class—collaboration metrics—addresses the degree to which the humans and automation are aware of one another and can adjust their behavior accordingly. As discussed above, effective collaborative teams are notable for their cohesion and flexibility. To achieve this state, it is not enough for people to understand their machine colleagues; machines should understand aspects of humans and their goals as well. Toward this end, machines need to model people in ways that capture their expectations, commands, and constraints and also be able to understand what people "say" (in whatever language—formal or natural—they are using). What does the human expect the computer to do? What is the human telling the computer to do? What

---

[13] See, for example, D. R. Olsen and M. A. Goodrich, 2003; A. Steinfeld et al., 2006; and J. Crandall and M. L. Cummings, 2007.

are constraints on the human, such as fatigue and bias, that might affect the human's behavior? Although machines that can "understand" humans in such ways are not typically found in current operational settings, relevant work is emerging from research laboratories. With increasing deployment of these features, automated parts of human-machine systems could modify their actions in response to human behavior and predicted states.

The human-automation collaboration metric revolves around measures of team cognition and trust. Evaluation of these parameters can inform system design requirements as well as the development of training material. Objective measurement of trust, a difficult task, is important when system reliability and a culture where different knowledge domains exist in distinct silos could create trust barriers.

In the automation-automation collaboration subclass, the quality and efficiency of the collaboration among the machines can be measured through metrics such as speed of data sharing and decision making among automated agents, quality of the system response to unexpected events, and the ability of the system to handle network disruptions.

The last collaboration metric subclass is human-human collaboration, also referred to as team collaboration. In networked settings, a human team necessarily works together to perform collaborative tasks, so performance should be measured at the holistic level rather than by aggregating team members' individual performance (Cooke et al., 2004). Because team members must consistently exchange information, reconcile inconsistencies, and coordinate their actions, one way to measure holistic team performance is through human-human coordination, which includes written, oral, and gestural interactions.

Human-human coordination is generally assessed through communication analysis, which can include quantitative physical measures such as how long team members spend communicating, as well as more qualitative measures that focus on the communication content. In addition, the measures can focus on a single point in time or they can address dynamic features, such as patterns of communication. Measures of behavioral patterns such as communications and social networks are traditional metrics in team research (Entin and Entin, 2001; Morrow and Fischer, 2013).

In addition to measuring team coordination for the human-human metric subclass, assessing team cognition, which refers to the thoughts and knowledge of the team, can be valuable in evaluating team performance and identifying effective training and design interventions (Fiore and Schooler, 2004). As efficient team performance has been shown to be related to the degree to which team members agree on, or are aware of task, role, and problem characteristics (Fiore and Schooler, 2004), team mental models and team situation awareness should be considered.

Determining which and how many metrics to gather depends on many details of a given situation. Designing a solution can occur only in the context of a specific system.

The metrics discussed in this section are intended to measure the first-order effects of human-autonomous system interaction, but they do not assess the larger sociotechnical impact of a technology and potential derivative effects. For example, when a new automated decision support tool is introduced into financial trading services, how the introduction of such a tool could affect market trading patterns is generally not known. Such behavior emerges after some time, with potential subsequent problem that must be addressed by regulatory agencies after the fact. Other examples might include the use of drones, which saves lives of the attackers but can kill innocent people and negatively impact attitudes of the affected population. Similarly, decisions about what kind of car to buy, or how far to live from work, can affect climate change, which is usually not consciously measured while such decisions are debated. What metrics can be used to capture the large-scale impacts of important decisions? We don't yet have strong capabilities for predicting the sociotechnical impacts of decisions and of how they could be measured, nor of accurately predicting how a system might develop. This is an open area of research and one that deserves more focus.

Chapter 5

ENABLING TECHNOLOGIES

Based on the components discussed in Chapters 3 and 4, it is becoming feasible to assemble human-computer teams that are suitable for some decision making. This chapter provides some background on the following research areas that underlie human-machine collaboration for decision making: sensing, software agent systems, neuroscience, and human computation. A good deal of innovation is taking place in these areas, but fundamental questions remain before the pieces can be assembled into reliable decision-making systems.

SENSING

When considering humans or animals, sensing often refers to the processes by which stimuli from outside or inside the body are received and felt, such as through the faculties of hearing, sight, smell, touch, taste, and equilibrium. Thus, sensing is a person's critical mechanism for data acquisition. The act of sensing as pure *data acquisition*—for example, translation of data from the world to the computer—has advanced significantly in recent years. Whereas data acquisition used to be the bottleneck for the data-to-decisions pipeline, that is no longer the case for many disciplines. It is because of these advances in data acquisition that we can now work on improving the entire data-to-decisions process.

Consider the volumes of images and video, a critical source of data for decision making by both humans and machines, which are now readily available. Users upload about 300 million images a day to Facebook,[1] with this number increasing to more than a billion a day during some special occasions.[2] Additional photo-sharing sites such as WhatsApp, Picasa, and Flickr add to this incredible source of imagery for decision making. Technological progress has made digital cameras so cheap (and advanced) that they are in the pockets of hundreds of millions of people, something unheard of just 10 years ago. Similarly, the Department of Defense acquires significant amounts of images and videos in daily operations, with reports indicating terabytes of data being generated in Iraq in a single day. Both Google and Facebook possess sufficient data for reliable object recognition, even face identification, at levels that rival human performance.[3] These are relatively simple tasks, but they offer clear examples of the value that large quantities of data bring to important applications. Similar examples can be found in fields such as medical diagnostics and other disciplines with very well-defined tasks and performance goals, although that degree of definition is not always possible in data-to-decision scenarios.

Analysis is clearly lagging behind sensing and data acquisition, even in cases where access to enormous amounts of data has improved (as in constrained object recognition, see more on this below). Still, progress has been made in recent years in the automatic analysis of vast amounts of sensed visual information, such as the analysis of consumer photographs, and in

---

[1] See http://www.businessinsider.com/facebook-images-a-day-instagram-acquisition-2012-7.
[2] See http://techcrunch.com/2013/01/17/facebook-photos-record/.
[3] See http://www.technologyreview.com/news/525586/facebook-creates-software-that-matches-faces-almost-as-well-as-you-do/.

automatic language translation, to name two popular capabilities used in the Internet. It is precisely the exploitation of large amounts of sensed data, more than the analysis of particular instances, that has been driving the interpretation of visual information. While it is not yet clear whether this is the only way to obtain state-of-the-art performance (and probably is not), access to large amounts of data has been found to be critical for learning visual features important for image and object recognition. Such automatic analysis is the only way to deal with massive amounts of data, and the only way to infer hidden information and singularities relevant for decision making. Significant recent examples in this area include, again, the automatic annotation and labeling (object detection) of millions of images by team of G. Hinton[4] (University of Toronto and Google), based on deep learning, and the development of technologies for assisting the visually impaired, such as the OrCam.[5] The outstanding performance of such technologies is clearly dependent on the ability to observe large amounts of data to learn the patterns needed. Such automatic analysis of image information is critical for decision making within systems such as those in an automobile that can automatically detect a pedestrian ahead and direct the car to stop.[6] The system developed by OrCam is a clear additional example of humans and sensing machines collaborating to make a decision (Do I cross the street? Do I sit at this table?), with the human first pointing the camera in an "interesting" direction, the machine (video camera or sensing device, and algorithms for automatic interpretation) providing information, and finally the human using such information for decision making.

In addition to sensing the visual world, data to decisions also depends on other modalities such as audio and text. Audio sensing and analysis has also significantly advanced in recent years, as we clearly witness from the automatic categorization of voice when users call service centers, something once again unheard of 10 years ago but now used with high reliability by multiple call centers. One of the most interesting advances in the area of "sensed text" is in automatic translation. While this is based on large amounts of data as well, it has critical components of grammatical structure, an area still lacking in the analysis of visual data, where the "grammar" of pictures is significantly lacking.

A critical new challenge resulting from the advance of sensing technology is its integration. This means not only understanding how to merge and combine different sensing disciplines but also understanding when and how one can replace or augment the other, in particular, when one is significantly cheaper or easier to deploy. For example, are functional MRIs necessary to understand brain activity and states of the human decision-making process, or can the same information be inferred (at least the information critical for understanding decision making) from simpler data acquisition devices such as eye tracking?

Sensing keeps improving, but it still faces numerous challenges, such as continuing to reduce the size and the energy consumption of sensing devices. Biologically inspired sensors constitute a very exciting area of research with significant advances almost daily. Our success in data acquisition has spawned a new challenge: developing the capability to eliminate the incredible amounts of uninformative data we acquire. We have clearly transitioned into the phase

---

[4] See, for example, Krizhevsky, A., I. Sustskever, and G. E. Hinton. ImageNet classification with deep convolutional neural networks. *Advances in Neural Information Processing 25,* MIT Press: Cambridge, MA, 2012.

[5] See http://www.nytimes.com/2013/06/04/science/israeli-start-up-gives-visually-impaired-a-way-to-read.html.

[6] See http://www.mobileye.com/.

where the challenge for many disciplines is in the automatic analysis and interpretation of the sensed world, and not so much on sensing it.

SOFTWARE AGENTS

Although there does not seem to be a universally acceptable definition of a software agent, the community of agent research and practice would generally agree that a software agent is a computational system that (a) is situated in an environment; (b) is goal directed; (c) is capable of flexible, autonomous action; and (d) learns from its experience.[7] Element (a) means that the agent is able to receive input from the real or the informational world and performs actions that could change its environment in some ways. "Autonomy" does not mean that the agent has complete ability to reason and act on its own, but that certain 'autonomous capabilities' may minimize the need for human supervision for particular tasks and task contexts;[8] and that the agent is able to control its internal computational state and actions. "Flexibility" means that the agent should be responsive (adaptive) to perceived changes in the environment. Additionally the agent is proactive; that is, the agent can exhibit goal-directed behavior, make predictions about future environment states, respond appropriately to the predictions, and take appropriate initiatives. The agent should be able to learn by its experiences, and thus improve its performance. Finally, the agent should be social; that is, able to interact with other artificial agents or humans in the course of performing its own problem solving or in order to assist others. In a multiagent system, each agent has incomplete information about the environment, other agents, their attitudes and problem-solving abilities; there is no overall system control (each agent controlling its problem solving locally); data is typically decentralized; and computation is asynchronous. Even though distributed computation offers robustness, in that there is no single point of system failure, multiagent systems face a multitude of challenges, including

- How to formulate the distributed problem, allocate tasks to various agents, and synthesize the results;
- How to initiate agent interactions, including when and what agents should communicate;
- How to ensure coherence in the distributed problem solving and avoid harmful interactions and effects;
- How to enable agents to reason about the state of their overall coordinated process;
- How to manage allocation of limited resources;
- How to allow agents to form and maintain a model of the other agents' problem solving so as to coordinate more effectively;
- How to reconcile conflicting local viewpoints, intentions, information, and results;
- How to manage distributed problem solving in the face of failures, and changing environmental and social dynamics (e.g., agents unpredictably leave and join the agent society); and

---

[7] This definition is adapted from Jennings, Sycara, and Wooldridge, 1998.
[8] See for example, Bradshaw, J.M, Robert R. Hoffman, Matthew Johnson, and David D. Woods. The Seven Deadly Myths of "Autonomous Systems." *IEEE Intelligent Systems*, May/June 2013 28:(3):54-61.

- How to manage asynchrony of communication and computation and determine effective trade-offs between communication and local computation, especially in the face of the increasing amount of data available to the multiagent system.

Research to date has identified and modeled a variety of multiagent coordination regimes. They range from teamwork,[9] where the agents work towards common goals, to adversarial interactions, where the agents would like to maximize their own payoffs even at the expense of other agents. Using different coordination regimes, a multitude of applications of single agents and multiagent systems have been developed in such diverse areas as manufacturing, electronic commerce, transportation, telecommunications, air traffic control, military and civilian crisis response, health management, games and entertainment, and information management. This latter application domain is most relevant to the data-to-decisions context, because it develops agents to manage the user's information overload problems[10] that arise from the vast volume of information available from a myriad of information-gathering systems.

Most of the applications alluded to above have involved software agents that collaborate without human interaction, or where the human interaction with the agent(s) is very simple and stylized. However, it is likely that with the increased sophistication of agent technology and network pervasiveness, agent support for decision making will (a) move beyond today's state, in which the agent involvement is relatively stylized and of short duration (e.g., buying a travel ticket) to more complex and longer-duration situations (e.g., assistance while driving) and (b) transition from assistance offered to a single decision maker to assistance offered to human-networked decision-making teams. While a large body of research has been conducted for agent decision support of single decision makers, there is comparatively little work on agent assistance for networked human decision-making teams.

AGENTS SUPPORTING HUMANS

Researchers desire to make agents an integral part of teams (Christoffersen and Woods, 2004), but this desire has not yet been fully realized. Researchers must identify how to best incorporate agents into human teams and what roles they should assume. The three primary roles that agents play when interacting with humans are as follows (Sycara and Lewis, 2004):

1. Agents supporting individual team members in completion of their own tasks. These agents often function as personal assistant agents and are assigned to specific team members. Two situations exist: either each human is supported by a single agent proxy in which agent proxies interact with other agents to accomplish the human's tasks, or each human is supported by a team of agents that work to accomplish the single human's directives. Often there are no other humans involved in the task, and

---

[9] Teamwork activities may include negotiation and auctions, where the agents interact in order to resolve conflicts (as in resource and task allocation), and formation of coalitions, where agents form alliances for more effective problem solving.

[10] Information overload problems include information gathering and selection (where the sheer amount of information present prevents the decision maker from finding the particular information he or she requires); information filtering of the enormous amounts of information that a decision maker is faced with; and information reconciliation and fusion.

the only "teamwork" involved is between the software agents. Examples of these type of agent systems include agents assisting humans in allocating disaster rescue resources and multi-robot control systems in which teams of robots perform tasks under the guidance of a human operator. Task-specific agents utilized by multiple team members also belong in this category.

2. Agents supporting the team as a whole. The performance of teams, especially in tightly coupled tasks, is believed to be highly dependent on the following interpersonal skills: information exchange, communication, supporting behavior, and team initiative and leadership. Therefore, agents supporting the team as a whole, rather than focusing on task-completion activities of individual human team members, directly facilitate teamwork by aiding communication, coordination among human agents, and focus of attention. In certain applications, this has shown to be more effective than having the agents directly aid in task completion (Sycara and Lewis, 2004). Aiding teamwork also requires less domain knowledge than aiding tasks, thus suggesting that teamwork aids might be reusable across domains. The experimental results summarized in Sycara and Lewis (2004) indicate that aiding human teamwork rather than individual team members might be the most effective aiding strategy for agents in support of human teams.

3. Agents assuming the role of an equal team member. These agents are expected to function as "virtual humans" within the organization, capable of the same reasoning and tasks as their human teammates (Traum et al., 2003). This is the hardest role for a software agent to assume, since it is difficult to create a software agent that is as effective as a human at both task performance and teamwork skills. Instead of merely assisting human team members, the software agents can assume equal roles in the team, sometimes replacing missing human team members. It can be challenging to develop software agents of comparable competency with human performers unless the task is relatively simple. Agents often fulfill this role in training simulation applications, acting as team members or tutors for the human trainees.[11]

RESEARCH CHALLENGES IN AGENT SUPPORT

Creating shared understanding between human and agent teammates is a sizable challenge facing developers of mixed-initiative collaborative human-agent systems. The limiting factor in most human-agent interactions is the user's ability and willingness to spend time communicating with the agent in a manner that both humans and agents understand, rather than the agent's computational power and bandwidth (Sycara and Lewis, 2004). The problem of shared understanding—whether the agents reduce uncertainty through communication, inference, or a mixture of the two—has been formulated (Horvitz, 1999) as a process of managing uncertainties: (1) managing uncertainties that agents may have about user's goals and focus of attention, and (2) uncertainty that users have about agent plans and status. Also, protecting users from unauthorized agent interactions is a concern in any application of agent technology.

---

[11] See, for example, Rickel and Johnson, 2003.

NEUROSCIENCE

Arguably, one of the areas that may hold the most promise for integrated teams of humans and machines truly acting as teammates is neuroscience. Neuroscience from the broadest perspective is the understanding of how the brain (and in particular the human brain) processes information, executes cognition and then takes actions based on that information. Across the animal kingdom, the human brain – with its dense and folded cortex – is seen to be the pinnacle of cognitive evolution. Our ability to experience, reason, remember and make decisions based on cause and effect is key to our dominance and success as a species. Although consciousness and decision making come naturally and easily to us in our daily lives, the precise biological mechanisms of cognition are not well understood. A great deal of outstanding fundamental research over the last three decades has given us a glimpse into the anatomical regions and cortical networks that underlie cognition. Recent advances in neuroscience and brain-sensing technology such as fMRI (functional magnetic resonance imaging) have allowed us to see inside the brain when we make decisions. For example, different labs are investigating brain activity, via fMRI, when making decisions,[12] providing a window (and a potential signal input) into still one of the most complicated decision systems available: the human mind. The signal can also be used to actually reconstruct and read the sensed world, in other words, reverse engineer the brain and understand the sensed image by looking at the (fMRI) signal.[13] However, it is just within the last decade that we are beginning to make strides on understanding the functioning of the human brain in more applied settings that deal with practical decision making and tasks of military and intelligence relevance.[14] Researchers are beginning to identify brain activities that are associated with decision making.[15] These measures are typically made in real-time, non invasively with electroencephalography (EEG). Some of these signals are subconscious and can occur before a person realizes that he or she has made a decision.[16] Other physiological activities, too, are coupled with decision making. Eye-tracking

---

[12] See http://sites.duke.edu/huettellab/; http://www.haririlab.com/home.html.

[13] See http://newscenter.berkeley.edu/2011/09/22/brain-movies/.

[14] See Kruse, A.A.: Operational neuroscience: neurophysiological measures in applied environments. *Aviat Space Environ Med.* 78(5), 4–191 (2007).

[15] See Macdonald, J., Mathan, S.P., and Yeung, N. (2011). Trial-by-trial variations in subjective attentional state are reflected in ongoing prestimulus EEG alpha oscillations. *Frontiers In Psychology*, 2 (82); Mathan, S., Erdogmus, D., Huang, C., Pavel, M., Ververs, P., Carciofini, J., Dorneich, M., and Whitlow, S. 2008. Rapid image analysis using neural signals. In CHI '08 *Extended Abstracts on Human Factors in Computing Systems,* (Florence, Italy, April 05 - 10, 2008). CHI '08. ACM, New York, NY, 3309-3314.

[16] See Sajda, P., Pohlmeyer, E., Wang, J., Parra, L. C., Christoforou, C., Dmochowski, J., et al. (2010). In a Blink of an Eye and a Switch of a Transistor: Cortically Coupled Computer Vision. *Proceedings of the IEEE*, 98(3), 462-478. doi:10.1109/JPROC.2009.2038406; Pohlmeyer, E. A., Wang, J., Jangraw, D. C., Lou, B., Chang, S.-F., and Sajda, P. (2011). Closing the loop in cortically-coupled computer vision: A brain-computer interface for searching image databases. *Journal of Neural Engineering*, 8(3), 036025. doi:10.1088/1741-2560/8/3/036025.

and pupillometry technologies are also very helpful in sensing our attention and are helping to understand how we scan (sense) the world before making decisions.[17]

In the work of Sajda et al. (2010), the real-time brain signatures are not only used to help the analyst perform the image triage task more quickly, but they are also used to train the assistive computer vision system. Over time, with the brain-in-the-loop and computational system as a team, the overall performance of the system will improve. Humans will be less overwhelmed with data, and the computational system will have learned from the ultimate expert. While these results have been seen most clearly in specific task domains (largely due to funding availability), we expect that as neurophysiological monitoring become more ubiquitous the implications will be much wider. Eventually, real-time neurophysiological responses for decision making could inform the computer in a way that enables the human to make better future decisions—perhaps even about physical manifestations of subconscious knowledge or levels of confidence. Similarly, another method for using this real-time information would be to feed back the individual's state to the user. In neurofeedback paradigms, self-awareness can enhance a person's ability to best manage his or her state, which may eventually include states related to optimal decision making. This approach has been demonstrated with physiological data in the Quantified Self community—and before long will also extend to cognition. Likewise, although early in development—are real-time neural measures of team cognition.[18] Research has demonstrated that optimally performing teams, on complex tasks like submarine navigation, can be detected from their collective brain signatures alone. Perhaps one day, the computer will join in the networked teams, both collaborating on a task and sensing/optimizing the performance of its human teammates. In additional to purely decision making states, research is now revealing brain states that may account for bias formation and influenceability.[19] Recent research has shown that persuasive messaging about how others feel about painful stimuli, can actually influence an individual's physical perception of how painful that stimulus is. (personal communication, DARPA Narrative Networks Program). Being able to detect or at least guard against bias and influence may be another role that neuroscience can play in this space.

The interactions described have been explicitly non-invasive, using only passively

---

[17] Decision-level fusion of EEG and pupil features for single-trial visual detection analysis. Ming Qian, Mario Aguilar, Karen N Zachery, Claudio Privitera, Stanley Klein, Thom Carney, Loren W Nolte; Teledyne Scientific and Imaging LLC, Research Triangle Laboratory, Durham, NC 27713, USA. *IEEE transactions on bio-medical engineering* (Impact Factor: 2.15). 04/2009; 56(7):1929-37. DOI:10.1109/TBME.2009.2016670. Marshall, S. P. (2007). Identifying cognitive state from eye metrics. *Aviation, Space, & Environmental Medicine*, 78(5), 165-175; Marshall, S. P. (2007). Measures of Attention and Cognitive Effort in Tactical Decision Making. In M. Cook, J. Noyes, & V. Masakowski (Eds.), *Decision Making in Complex Environments* (pp. 321-332). Aldershot, Hampshire UK: Ashgate Publishing;

[18] See Stevens R., Galloway T., Wang P., Berka C., Tan V., Wohlgemuth T., Lamb J., and Buckles R. (2012). Modeling the neurodynamic complexity of submarine navigation team. *Computational and Mathematical Organization Theory*, August 2012; DOI 10.1007/s10588-012-9135-9; Kovacs, A., Tognoli, E., Afergan, D., Coyne, J., Gibson, G., Stripling, J., Keso, J.A.S.: Brain Dynamics of Coordinated Teams. In: *Human Computer Interaction International*, Orlando, FL. Springer, Heidelberg (2011).

[19] See Falk, E.B., O'Donnell, M.B., & Lieberman (2012). Getting the word out: Neural correlates of enthusiastic message propagation. *Frontiers in Human Neuroscience*, 6:313; Falk, E.B., Berkman, E.T., Mann, T. Harrison, B., & Lieberman, M.D. (2010). Predicting persuasion-induced behavior change from the brain. *Journal of Neuroscience*, 30, 8421-8424.

recorded signals on the surface of the scalp or functional imaging with magnets. The signals are measured in response to the human completing a task or engaging in a specific mental exercise. In contrast to passive recording, brain-computer interfaces (BCI) provide a direct avenue of communication between the human brain and an external device. So far, much of the work in this area has focused on medical applications—for example, restoration of missing sensory capabilities. Enormous progress has been made in this area for prosthetics and motor controls for locked-in patients; however, there has been little utility to date for direct BCI in every-day task settings. In reality this is because for most able-bodied individuals, motor actions are much faster and more precise than those translated through BCI mechanisms. BCI approaches, particularly those that do not require implantation of electrodes in the surface of the brain, require extensive training and are highly specific to the individual. In principle, it might be possible to exploit progress in this field for decision making. For example, Chapter 3 mentioned the possibility of using machines to help humans consider new alternatives and to reduce errors. In that context, the text was referring to devices that would prod people from outside their bodies. It is conceivable, however, that computer algorithms might one day enhance the quality of human deliberation through direct interaction with the brain. Similarly, they might extend human memory or provoke "out-of-the-box" thinking. Already there is a robust collection of transcranial direct current stimulation (tDCS) research in cognition and neuroscience.[20] In tDCS a simple device is used to inject a weak electrical current into the brain through the scalp. This method has not yet entered main stream paradigms for performance enhancement. However, as these devices become readily accessible to consumers (www.foc.us), we may see practical applications emerge before the research community

Seamless computer-brain connections might not only supply "extra intelligence" to humans, as fantasized about in the paragraph above. This technology might also allow people to control machines with their thoughts.

Both investment in and further study of these applied questions in neuroscience will certainly inform the future of decision making, particularly as envisioned in this study. As neurophysiological and physiological monitoring becomes more commonplace in the work environment, researchers and engineers will leverage these inputs for increased performance across the entire decision making system. Whether that is harnessing the natural talents of the human brain, aiding the decision maker through feedback on workload or bias, or eventually participating fully in an integrated team—the network of human and computation will play a key role in these future systems.

---

[20]See for example, Manuel A.L., David, A.W., Bikson, M., Schnider, A. Frontal tDCS modulates orbitofrontal reality filtering. *Neuroscience* 2014; 264: 21-27; Berker, A.O., Bikson, M., Bestmann, S. Predicting the behavioural impact of transcranial direct current stimulation: issues and limitations Frontiers of Human Neuroscience 2013; Transcranial direct current stimulation's effect on novice versus experienced learning. Bullard, L.M., Browning, E.S., Clark, V.P., Coffman, B.A., Garcia, C.M., Jung, R.E, van der Merwe, A.J., Paulson, K.M., Vakhtin, A.A., Wootton, C.L., Weisend, M.P. *Exp Brain Res.* 2011 Aug;213(1):9-14. doi: 10.1007/s00221-011-2764-2. Epub 2011 June 26.

HUMAN COMPUTATION

Although computers are of course well known for their computational powers, humans have some unique strengths in this arena. Human computation, such as crowdsourcing, is "a new and evolving research area that centers around harnessing human intelligence to solve computational problems that are beyond the scope of existing Artificial Intelligence (AI) algorithms" (Law and von Ahn, 2011).

The Association for the Advancement of Artificial Intelligence has recognized this potential: It held its first conference on the topic in November 2013 (humancomputation.com/2013/). The organization invited submissions on "efforts and developments on principles, experiments, and implementations of systems that rely on programmatic access to human intellect to perform some aspect of computation, or where human perception, knowledge, reasoning, or physical activity and coordination contributes to the operation of larger computational systems, applications, and services."

Quinn and Bederson (2011) make a distinction between human computation and crowdsourcing. They consider human computation to refer to replacing computers with humans, and "crowdsourcing" to mean "replacing traditional human workers with members of the public." However, many other researchers use the terms interchangeably, as we do here.

A recent report from the National Research Council[21] discussed the use of human computation, or crowdsourcing, for data acquisition, noting that "This has already been shown to be a powerful mechanism for tasks as varied as monitoring road traffic, identifying and locating distributed phenomena, and discovering emerging trends and events." It points to tasks such as "deep language understanding and certain kinds of pattern recognition and outlier detection" that can be performed better by people than by machines, and notes a number of emerging opportunities to harness that capability. It goes on to make a distinction between crowdsourcing that leverages human activity, such as by tracking the way humans search for information on the Web or navigate a challenge, and that which leverages human intelligence, such as by enlisting multiple humans to work in parallel to label images or otherwise contribute to content and analyses.

That same report identified several types of crowdsourced systems that apply to data analysis:

> • *User-generated content sites*. Wikipedia is a prominent example of a user-generated content site where people create, modify, and update pages of information about a huge range of topics. More specialized sites exist for reviews and recommendations of movies, restaurants, products, and so on. In addition to creating basic content, in many of these systems users are also able to edit and curate the data, resulting in collections of data that can be useful in many analytics tasks.
>
> • *Task platforms*. Much of the interest around crowdsourcing has been focused on an emerging set of systems known as microtask platforms. A microtask platform creates a marketplace in which requesters offer tasks and workers accept and perform the tasks. Microtasks usually do not require any special training and typically

---

[21] For more information see, National Research Council, *Frontiers in Massive Data Analysis,* National Academies Press, Washington, DC., 2013, pp. 137-138.

take no longer than 1 minute to complete, although they can take longer. Typical microtasks include labeling images, cleaning and verifying data, locating missing information, and performing subjective or context-based comparisons. One of the leading platforms at present is Amazon Mechanical Turk (AMT). In AMT, workers from anywhere in the world can participate, and there are thought to be hundreds of thousands of people who perform jobs on the system.

Other task-oriented platforms have been developed or proposed to do more sophisticated work. For example, specialized platforms have been developed to crowdsource creative work such as designing logos (e.g., 99designs) or writing code (e.g., TopCoder). In addition, some groups have developed programming languages to encode more sophisticated multistep tasks, such as Turkit (Little et al., 2010), or market-based mechanisms for organizing larger tasks (Shahaf and Horvitz, 2010). These types of platforms can be used to get human participation on a range of analytics tasks, from simple disambiguation to more sophisticated iterative processing.

• *Crowdsourced query processing*. Recently, a number of research efforts have investigated the integration of crowdsourcing with query processing as performed by relational database systems. Traditional database systems are limited in their ability to tolerate inconsistent or missing information, which has restricted the domains in which they can be applied largely to those with structured, fairly clean information. Crowdsourcing based on application programming interfaces (APIs) provides an opportunity to engage humans to help with those tasks that are not sufficiently handled by database systems today. CrowdDB (Franklin et al., 2011) and Qurk (Marcus et al., 2011) are examples of such experimental systems.

• *Question-answering systems*. Question-answering systems are another type of system for enlisting human intelligence. Many different kinds of human-powered or human-assisted sites have been developed. These include general knowledge sites where humans help answer questions (e.g., Cha Cha), general expertise-based sites, where people with expertise in particular topics answer questions on those topics (e.g., Quora), and specialized sites focused on a particular topic (e.g., StackOverflow for computer-programming related questions).

• *Massive multi-player online games*. Another type of crowdsourcing site uses gamification to encourage people to contribute to solving a problem. Such games can be useful for simulating complex social systems, predicting events (e.g., prediction markets), or for solving specific types of problems. One successful example of the latter type of system is the FoldIt site [http://fold.it], where people compete to most accurately predict the way that certain proteins will fold. FoldIt has been competitive with, and in some cases even beaten, the best algorithms for protein folding, even though many of the people participating are not experts.

- *Specialized platforms.* Some crowdsourcing systems have been developed and deployed to solve specialized types of problems. One example is Ushahidi [http://ushahidi.com], which provides geographic-based information and visualizations for crisis response and other applications. Another such system is Galaxy Zoo [http://www.galaxyzoo.org], which enables people to help identify interesting objects in astronomical images. Galaxy Zoo learns the skill sets of its participants over time and uses this knowledge to route particular images to the people who are most likely to accurately detect the phenomena in those images.

- *Collaborative analysis.* This class of systems consists of the crowdsourcing platforms that are perhaps the most directly related to data analytics at present. Such systems enable groups of people to share and discuss data and visualizations in order to detect and understand trends and anomalies. Such systems typically include a social component in which participants can directly engage each other. Examples of such systems include ManyEyes, Swivel, and Sense.us.[22]

Other useful overviews of this topic include E. Kamar, et al. (Combining Human and Machine Intelligence in Large-scale Crowdsourcing, AAMAS 2012, 2012; http://research.microsoft.com/pubs/162286/galaxyZoo.pdf) and D. Shahaf, et al. (Generalized Task Markets for Human and Machine Computation, AAAI 2010. http://www.aaai.org/ocs/index.php/AAAI/AAAI10/paper/viewFile/1951/2132). While the area of human computation is still quite new, the wide range of innovation currently emerging seems likely to someday produce results that can be applied to complex decision making.

---

[22] Extended quote taken from pp. 139-141 of *Frontiers in Massive Data Analysis*, National Research Council, National Academies Press, Washington, DC, 2013.

Chapter 6

CONCLUSION

Although it is likely that human-computer decision-making systems will continue to advance, a complete path forward is not yet clear. As illustrated in this report, important progress is being made in a number of underlying technologies and scientific foundations, and in particular there is a good deal of innovation in human-computing interfaces. However, the committee identified three general challenges:

1. Scientists do not fully understand the human decision-making process. That understanding is being built up in multiple fields, such as cognitive science, cultural anthropology, decision science, neuroscience, and psychology. Without a more complete understanding of how humans decide, it is difficult to know how far advances in human-machine decision making can go. We do not know all the enablers of good decisions and how those enablers might be turned against us. What is the likely progress for those enablers over the next 20 years, and what are the metrics to track in order to discern progress? Are others likely to move ahead of the U.S. on any of these enablers? How can we integrate all these enablers in order to improve data-to-decisions? All of these fundamental questions require further investigation.
2. There is no "silver bullet." Enhancing human-machine collaboration does not solely depend on finding the right algorithms, or on improving computerized language processing, or on designing a more natural interface between humans and machines, or on resolving challenges associated with "big data" and so forth. Rather, all of these solutions and more are needed. Indeed, although this report touches on 11 different fields and subfields,[1] these represent just some of the scientific approaches that could be included to enhance human-machine collaboration for decision making. While the problem is profoundly multidisciplinary, university departments—both in the United States and elsewhere—are still largely focused on individual fields. Even in those universities where exciting multidisciplinary research is conducted there are limits to how far researchers tend to go outside their own subject matter, such as learning, critiquing, and adopting one another's terminology and concepts. It is possible that public or public-private institutions, such as the Agency for Science Technology and Research and the German Research Centre for Artificial Intelligence (described in Appendix B), may offer innovative approaches to interdisciplinary research.
3. There is a need to better understand the social implications of human-machine collaboration for decision making.[2] Whether machines ought to "decide" when to pull the trigger has been

---

[1] Artificial intelligence, cognitive science, computer science, data analytics, decision science, machine learning, natural language processing, neuroscience, psychology, statistics, systems engineering.

[2] A useful discussion of these issues may be found in *Emerging and Readily Available Technologies and National Security—A Framework for Addressing Ethical, Lethal and Societal Issues*. National Academies Press, 2014.

discussed broadly.[3] But as machines become better decision makers, will humans increasingly defer to them? Should they? What will happen to human cognitive processes as humans gain greater fluency with computing, especially through early childhood formal and informal learning? How should the need for privacy (by the government as well as the individual) be assessed relative to the ability to fully harness the potential benefits of data sharing?

The committee identified a number of promising research directions to improve the scientific basis for strong human-computer decision making and to help inform these open challenges:

- Data-to-decisions is an umbrella term that is not clearly defined. We need a better understanding of how cognitive functions can be supported over time and in context and an overall framework for thinking about how to design human-computer decision systems; The ubiquitous capability to capture, store, reproduce, move, and reuse data has led to decisions increasingly being made by networks composed of humans and machines. Yet, the exploitation of that data is often ad hoc. Research is needed to frame and systematize how we exploit that data;
- At any moment, whether a particular datum will be relevant or irrelevant into the future is task and context dependent, so there is an incentive to retain more, rather than less. Thus, a key challenge is to build task and context models that enable data to be filtered and processed into "useful information";
- Another challenge is developing systems that allow both humans and computers to work together in a harmonious team, rather than one supervising the other. This requires research to help individual and team exploration of (partial and incomplete) hypotheses, to enable continuous learning by the system (e.g., so the system can learning how to predict an analyst's needs and preferences, to guide continuous ingesting of data and its metadata and fusing it into the existing data, to cue decision makers to relevant, unexplored data or behavior; and to facilitate the sharing of hypotheses and derived knowledge among team members (such as by developing languages that make it easy for decision makers to state what they want the data to tell them). Creating harmonious human-computer teams would also be helped by research in comparing the different roles of humans and computers in mixed teams;
- Complex decision making often takes place in a complex environment, with multiple activities occurring simultaneously. This leads to frequent interruptions and the need to switch tasks and revise priorities. Current human-computer systems do not handle interruptions well and they need to provide more support for the resumption of interrupted activities. More research is needed on computational interruption management techniques and algorithms, rooted in an understanding of people's cognitive and attentional capabilities; and
- More work is needed to develop a methodology for evaluating and assigning metrics for each individual piece of the collaboration and for the quality of the decisions made by the overall human-machine collaborative system.

---

[3] The numerous articles about the use of drones in military combat are just one example.

CONCLUSION

The committee members found more questions than answers during the course of this study. Their observations, however, do not call into doubt the importance of future human-machine collaboration for complex decision making as much as they underscore a present-day reality: The development of human-machine collaboration for complex decision making is still in its infancy relative to where cross-disciplinary research could take it over the next generation.

Appendix A

COMMITTEE BIOGRAPHIES

Committee on Integrating Humans, Machines and Networks:
A Global Review of Data-to-Decision Technologies

JACQUES S. GANSLER (Chair)
Dr. Jacques S. Gansler joined the faculty of the University of Maryland School of Public Affairs in 2001, where he holds the Roger C. Lipitz Chair in Public Policy and Private Enterprise. He teaches graduate school courses, and leads the school's new Center for Public Policy and Private Enterprise, which fosters collaboration among the public, private, and nonprofit sectors in order to promote mutually beneficial public and private interests. Previously, Dr. Gansler served as the under secretary of defense for acquisition, technology and logistics from November 1997 until January 2001. In this position, he was responsible for all matters relating to Department of Defense acquisition, research and development, logistics, acquisition reform, advanced technology, international programs, environmental security, nuclear, chemical, and biological programs, and the defense technology and industrial base. Prior to this appointment, Dr. Gansler was senior vice president and corporate director for TASC, Incorporated, an applied information technology company, in Arlington, Virginia (from 1977 to 1997), during which time he played a major role in building the company from a small operation into a large, widely recognized corporation, serving both the government and the private sector. From 1972 to 1977, he served in the government as deputy assistant secretary of defense (materiel acquisition), responsible for all defense procurements and the defense industry; and as assistant director of defense research and engineering (electronics), responsible for all defense electronics research and development. His prior industrial experience included vice president (business development), I.T.T. (1970–1972); program management, director of advanced programs, and director of international marketing, Singer Corporation (1962–1970); and engineering management, Raytheon Corporation (1956–1962). Dr. Gansler has served on numerous corporation boards of directors and governmental special committees and advisory boards, including vice chairman, Defense Science Board; chairman, Board of Visitors, Defense Acquisition University; director, Procurement Round Table; chairman, Industry Advisory Board, University of Virginia, School of Engineering; chairman, Board of Visitors, University of Maryland, School of Public Affairs; member of the Federal Aviation Administration Blue Ribbon Panel on Acquisition Reform; and senior consultant to the Packard Commission on defense acquisition reform. Additionally, from 1984 to 1997, Dr. Gansler was a visiting scholar at the Kennedy School of Government, Harvard University (a frequent guest lecturer in executive management courses). He is the author of 5 books, a contributing author of 23 other books, author of more than 100 papers, and a frequent speaker and congressional witness. Dr. Gansler is a member of the National Academy of Engineering. He holds a B.E. in electrical engineering from Yale University, an M.S. in electrical engineering from Northeastern University, an M.A. in political economy from the New School for Social Research, and a Ph.D. in economics from American University.

MARY (MISSY) CUMMINGS

Dr. Cummings received her B.S. in Mathematics from the US Naval Academy in 1988, her M.S. in Space Systems Engineering from the Naval Postgraduate School in 1994, and her Ph.D. in Systems Engineering from the University of Virginia in 2004. A naval officer and military pilot from 1988-1999, she was one of the Navy's first female fighter pilots. She is currently an associate professor in the Duke University Department of Mechanical Engineering and Materials Science, the Duke Institute of Brain Sciences, and is the director of the Humans and Autonomy Laboratory. Her research interests include human-unmanned vehicle interaction, human-autonomous system collaboration, human-systems engineering, public policy implications of unmanned vehicles, and the ethical and social impact of technology.

BARBARA J. GROSZ

Dr. Barbara Grosz is Higgins Professor of Natural Sciences in the School of Engineering and Applied Sciences at Harvard University. From 2007 to 2011, she served as interim dean and then dean of Harvard's Radcliffe Institute for Advanced Study, and from 2001 to 2007, she was the institute's first dean of science, designing and building its science program. Dr. Grosz is known for her seminal contributions to the fields of natural-language processing and multiagent systems. She developed some of the earliest computer dialogue systems and established the research field of computational modeling of discourse. Her work on models of collaboration helped establish that field and provides the framework for several collaborative multiagent and human-computer interface systems. Dr. Grosz is also known for her leadership in the field of artificial intelligence and her role in the establishment and leadership of interdisciplinary institutions, and she is widely respected for her contributions to the advancement of women in science.

Dr. Grosz is a member of the National Academy of Engineering, the American Philosophical Society, and the American Academy of Arts and Sciences and a fellow of the Association for the Advancement of Artificial Intelligence (AAAI), the Association for Computing Machinery (ACM), and the American Association for the Advancement of Science. In 2009, she received the ACM/AAAI Allen Newell Award for "fundamental contributions to research in natural language processing and in multi-agent systems, for her leadership in the field of artificial intelligence, and for her role in the establishment and leadership of interdisciplinary institutions."

ANITA JONES

Dr. Anita Jones has been a researcher and educator in computer science first at Carnegie Mellon University and then at the University of Virginia, where she was granted the title of University Professor. From 1993 to 1997, she served at the U.S. Department of Defense as director of defense research and engineering with oversight of the department's science and technology program, research laboratories, and the Defense Advanced Research Projects Agency. She served as vice chair of the National Science Board. Dr. Jones is a fellow of the Defense Science Board, the Association for Computing Machinery, the Institute of Electrical and Electronics Engineers (IEEE), and the Association for the Advancement of Science (AAAS). She is currently a member of the Charles Stark Draper Laboratory Corporation, a member of the MIT

Corporation, a trustee of Science Foundation Arizona, and a trustee of In-Q-Tel. Dr. Jones serves on the Executive Council of the National Academy of Engineering and the Governing Board of the National Research Council. Several awards have honored her accomplishments in science, technology, and national policy, including the National Academy of Engineering's Arthur M. Bueche Award (2010); the AAAS's highest award, the Philip Hague Abelson Award (2012); and the IEEE's Founder's Medal (2007). Dr. Jones earned a bachelor's degree in mathematics from Rice University, a master's in literature from the University of Texas, and a doctoral degree in computer science from Carnegie Mellon University.

AMY A. KRUSE
Dr. Amy Kruse joined Intific in January 2010 as an executive director, forming their new Neuroscience Division. She has recently led the release of their first commercial product, the RealWorld with NeuroBridge software platform. She also directs active Intific programs with the Office of Naval Research (team neurogaming), the Defense Advanced Research Projects Agency (DARPA) (ENGAGE, NowTu, Narrative Networks, Detection and Computational Analysis of Psychological Signals, Social Media in Strategic Communication), and the intelligence community. Dr. Kruse has more than 10 years of experience developing novel neuroscience-based programs and technologies for the Department of Defense. From January 2005 to January 2010, Dr. Kruse served as a program manager in the Defense Sciences Office at DARPA in Arlington, Virginia. During her tenure at DARPA, Dr. Kruse managed more than nine programs, including efforts in the Augmented Cognition, Neurotechnology for Intelligence Analysts, Accelerated Learning, and Cognitive Technology Threat Warning Systems programs, among others. Prior to DARPA, Dr. Kruse served as a technology and program management consultant at Strategic Analysis Inc. in Arlington, Virginia. During her time with SAINC, she provided hands-on technical assistance to nascent neuroscience programs at DARPA, the Office of Naval Research, and the Naval Research labs. She has been actively involved in neuroscience research for more than 15 years. Dr. Kruse earned her B.S. in cell and structural biology (1995) and her Ph.D. in neuroscience (2001) from the University of Illinois at Champaign-Urbana, where she was awarded a National Science Foundation Graduate Fellowship in Neuroscience.

GEORGE R. MANGUN
Dr. George R. Mangun is dean of the Division of Social Sciences, and professor of psychology and neurology in the Center for Mind and Brain at the University of California (UC), Davis. Dr. Mangun, an international leader in cognitive neuroscience, has taught and conducted research at UC San Diego, Dartmouth College, Duke University, and UC Davis. He was the founding director of the Duke Center for Cognitive Neuroscience, and the UC Davis Center for Mind and Brain. Dr. Mangun was editor of *Cognitive Brain Research* (Elsevier), and is currently associate editor for the *Journal of Cognitive Neuroscience* (MIT Press) and editor-in-chief for the edited book series *The Neuroscience of Attention* (Oxford University Press). He has and continues to serve on editorial boards, advisory committees, and review panels nationally and internationally, including for the National Institutes of Health, the National Science Foundation, the National Research Council of the U.S. National Academies, and the European Research Council. Dr. Mangun is currently the director of the National Institute of Mental Health (NIMH) Summer Institute in Cognitive Neuroscience. He has published more than 130 scientific papers, chapters, books, edited volumes, and special journal issues, including his celebrated coauthored undergraduate textbook *Cognitive Neuroscience: The Biology of the Mind* (W. W. Norton, 3rd

Edition, 2009). His research incorporates cognitive neuroscience methods in the study of the mechanisms of attention and awareness in health and disease using human volunteers and animal models. Among other honors, he received the Distinguished Early Career Contributions Award from the Society for Psychophysiological Research, a Distinguished Scientist Lecturer Award from the American Psychological Association, and a Senior Scientist Award from NIMH. Mangun is a fellow of the Association for Psychological Science and the American Association for the Advancement of Science.

TOM MITCHELL
Dr. Tom Mitchell is the chair of the Machine Learning Department at Carnegie Mellon University and E. Fredkin Professor of AI and Learning. Dr. Mitchell is known for his contributions to the advancement of machine learning, artificial intelligence, and cognitive neuroscience and is the author of the textbook *Machine Learning*. He received his bachelor of science degree in electrical engineering from the Massachusetts Institute of Technology in 1973 and a Ph.D. from Stanford University in 1979. He was elected to the National Academy of Engineering in 2010 "for pioneering contributions and leadership in the methods and applications of machine learning." He is also a fellow of the American Association for the Advancement of Science since 2008 and a fellow of the Association for the Advancement of Artificial Intelligence since 1990. Dr. Mitchell was also a recipient of the National Science Foundation's Presidential Young Investigator Award in 1984.

SEE-KIONG NG
Dr. See-Kiong Ng is program director of the Urban Systems Initiative of Singapore's Agency of Science, Technology and Research (A*STAR). The initiative seeks to address the new challenges of the rapidly urbanizing world through technology and innovation. Dr. Ng also holds a concurrent appointment as a principal scientist and the advisor to the Data Analytics Department at A*STAR's Institute for Infocomm Research. Before joining A*STAR, Dr. Ng worked as a postdoc at Keio University in Japan, as a senior investigator at SmithKline Beecham in England, and at DNA Sciences, a Silicon Valley biotech start-up in the United States. In 1986, Dr. Ng was awarded the prestigious Singapore National Computer Board's Overseas Scholarship. He holds a B.S., M.S., and Ph.D. in computer science from Carnegie Mellon University (1989, 1994, and 1998) and an M.S. in computer science from the University of Pennsylvania (1991).

DONALD A. NORMAN
Dr. Donald A. Norman is Director and founder of the Design at UC San Diego initiative, cofounder of the Nielsen Norman Group, former vice president of Apple, and former executive at Hewlett Packard. Dr. Norman serves as an IDEO fellow and is on several company boards and advisory boards. In addition to his role as Director of the design initiative, he is professor emeritus at the University of California, San Diego, where he served as chair of the Psychology Department and founder and chair of the Cognitive Science Department. At Northwestern University, he is the Breed Professor of Design, emeritus, and professor of electrical engineering and computer sciences, emeritus. He has been a Distinguished Visiting Professor of Industrial Design at the Korea Advanced Institute of Science and Technology. He has honorary degrees from the University of Padua (Italy) and the Technical University of Delft (the Netherlands), the Lifetime Achievement Award from SIGCHI, the professional organization for Computer-Human

Interaction, and the Benjamin Franklin Medal in Computer and Cognitive Science from the Franklin Institute (Philadelphia). He is a member of the National Academy of Engineering, and fellow of the American Academy of Arts and Sciences, Association for Computing Machinery, American Psychological Association, Association for Psychological Science, Human Factors and Ergonomics Society, and the Design Research Society. He serves on the Board of Trustees of the Illinois Institute of Technology's Institute of Design in Chicago. He is well known for his books, including Things That Make Us Smart and Design of Future Things, both of which dealt with the topics in this report. His books Emotional Design and the newly revised and expanded edition of Design of Everyday Things have been important contributions to the field of human-machine interaction.

GUILLERMO R. SAPIRO
Dr. Guillermo R. Sapiro received his B.S. (summa cum laude), M.S., and Ph.D. from the Department of Electrical Engineering at the Technion—Israel Institute of Technology in 1989, 1991, and 1993, respectively. After postdoctoral research at the Massachusetts Institute of Technology, Dr. Sapiro became Member of Technical Staff at the research facilities of Hewlett Packard Labs in Palo Alto, California. He was with the Department of Electrical and Computer Engineering at the University of Minnesota, where he held the position of Distinguished McKnight University Professor and Vincentine Hermes-Luh Chair in Electrical and Computer Engineering. Currently he is the Edmund T. Pratt, Jr. School Professor at Duke University. Dr. Sapiro works on the foundations of image processing with applications ranging from consumer imaging to neurosurgery. He has published more than 200 peer-reviewed papers and has transferred technology to companies such as Adobe as well as to neuroscientists and Department of Defense and National Institutes of Health sites. Dr. Sapiro was awarded the Gutwirth Scholarship for Special Excellence in Graduate Studies in 1991, the Ollendorff Fellowship for Excellence in Vision and Image Understanding Work in 1992, the Rothschild Fellowship for Post-Doctoral Studies in 1993, the Office of Naval Research Young Investigator Award in 1998, the Presidential Early Career Awards for Scientists and Engineers in 1998, the National Science Foundation Career Award in 1999, and the National Security Science and Engineering Faculty Fellowship in 2010. Dr. Sapiro is the founding editor-in-chief of the *SIAM Journal on Imaging Sciences*.

ROSS D. SHACHTER
Dr. Ross Shachter is associate professor of management science and engineering at Stanford University. He joined Stanford's faculty directly after receiving his Ph.D. degree. His doctoral dissertation developed a method for purchasing an expert's forecast that encourages accurate revelation of the expert's beliefs as probabilities. Since then his research has focused on the representation, manipulation, and analysis of uncertainty and probabilistic reasoning in decision systems. As part of this work, he developed the DAVID influence diagram processing system for the Macintosh. He has developed models scheduling patients for cancer follow-up, and analyzing vaccination strategies for HIV and *Helobacter pylori*. He has worked closely with many students in bioinformatics, where he holds a courtesy appointment. He has been active in the Conference on Uncertainty in Artificial Intelligence and is a full member of the Institute for Operations Research and the Management Sciences and its Decision Analysis Society. He has

held memberships in the American Association for Artificial Intelligence, the Society for Medical Decision Making, and the Society for Decision Professionals.

JAMES D. SHIELDS
Mr. Jim Shields is the president and chief executive officer of the Charles Stark Draper Laboratory, an independent not-for-profit research institution that develops innovative solutions to some of the nation's most difficult problems in national security and space. The laboratory also supports pioneering collaborations between traditional engineers and life scientists to demonstrate the value of biomedical engineering in creating systems solutions to health care problems that would not evolve if the disciplines worked independently. Previously, Mr. Shields was the vice president for programs, where he was responsible for developing and executing the laboratory's business and strategic plans. In addition to his operational role at Draper, Mr. Shields has supported a number of senior advisory boards and study panels, including the Defense Science Board, the Army Science Board, and the Navy Strategic Systems Programs Executive Steering Task Group as a board member, and the Air Force Scientific Advisory Board as a study participant. Prior to joining Draper in February 2001, Mr. Shields had a 28-year career at TASC, Inc., distinguished by a series of positions of increasing scope and responsibility. His final position was as the vice president for strategic development, where he was responsible for the planning process and the creation of TASC's strategic plans. His technical experience includes integrated multisensor navigation analysis, modeling and simulation, weapon system performance analysis, information management systems development, and logistics management. He earned S.B. and S.M. degrees in electrical engineering from MIT in 1972. He is a fellow of the American Institute of Aeronautics and Astronautics, a senior member of the Institute of Electrical and Electronics Engineers, and a member of Tau Beta Pi and Eta Kappa Nu.

LIZ SONENBERG
Dr. Liz Sonenberg is a professor in the Department of Computing and Information Systems at the University of Melbourne, and since August 2009, she has also had the part-time role of pro vice-chancellor (research collaboration) in Melbourne Research. The integrating theme of her research is the conceptualization and construction of more adaptive, distributed, and intelligent information systems. Much of the work focuses on agent technology, which views a distributed system in terms of interacting autonomous software entities. Using the agent metaphor can allow system developers to adopt a level of abstraction in design that is useful for modeling complex tasks and environments, and in building software systems that are robust in the face of change and unexpected events. An important aspect of the research is the requirement of the human-machine interface and consequent implications for the development of computational mechanisms to support decision making in complex settings. Her specialized interests are multiagent systems, especially collaboration and teamwork; automated negotiation and decision support; context-aware computing and technologies for personalization; and computational modeling of human problem solving.

KATIA SYCARA
Dr. Katia Sycara is a research professor in the School of Computer Science at Carnegie Mellon University and holds the Sixth Century Chair in Computing Science (part time) at the University of Aberdeen in the United Kingdom. She holds a Ph.D. in computer science from Georgia Tech

and an honorary doctorate from the University of the Aegean. Her research emphasis is on multiagent systems, composed of humans, robots, and software agents, and semantic web technologies. She has authored or coauthored more than 450 scientific publications and received many best paper and influential paper awards. She is a fellow of the Institute of Electrical and Electronics Engineers, fellow of the Association for the Advancement of Artificial Intelligence, and the recipient of the 2002 ACM/SIGART Autonomous Agents Research Award. She has served as a member of scientific advisory boards of many industrial research organizations and has been a member of evaluation panels of various government institutes and programs. She has also served on standards committees, for example, the World Wide Web Consortium and OASIS. She has served as program chair for many conferences and on numerous conference program committees. She is a founding member and member of the Board of Directors of the International Foundation of Multi-Agent Systems, founding member of the Semantic Web Science Association, and serves as the U.S. cochair of the U.S.-Europe Semantic Web Services Initiative. She has been a founding editor-in-chief of the journal *Autonomous Agents and Multi-Agent Systems* and serves on the editorial board of six additional journals.

ALYSON WILSON
Dr. Alyson Wilson is associate professor in the Department of Statistics at North Carolina State University (NCSU). She is a fellow of the American Statistical Association and a recognized expert in statistical reliability, Bayesian methods, and the application of statistics to problems in defense and national security. Prior to joining NCSU, Dr. Wilson was a research staff member at the Institute for Defense Analyses Science and Technology Policy Institute (2012–2013) and an associate professor in the Department of Statistics at Iowa State University (2008–2011). She continues as a collaborating associate professor with ISU and a guest scientist at Los Alamos National Laboratory. From 1999 to 2008, she was a project leader and technical lead for the Department of Defense Programs in the Statistical Sciences Group at Los Alamos National Laboratory. In this role, she developed and led a portfolio of work in the application of statistics to the reliability of conventional and nuclear weapons. Prior to her move to Los Alamos, Dr. Wilson was a senior operations research analyst with Cowboy Programming Resources (1995–1999), where she planned, executed, and analyzed U.S. Army air defense artillery operational evaluations. In addition to numerous publications, Dr. Wilson recently coauthored a book, *Bayesian Reliability*, and has coedited two other books, *Statistical Methods in Counterterrorism: Game Theory, Modeling, Syndromic Surveillance, and Biometric Authentication* and *Modern Statistical and Mathematical Methods in Reliability*. She holds a patent for her early work in medical imaging. Dr. Wilson received her Ph.D. in statistics from Duke University, her M.S. in statistics from Carnegie Mellon University, and her B.A. in mathematical sciences from Rice University.

Appendix B

INTERNATIONAL VISITS

The purpose of visiting labs outside the United States was to provide the sponsor with a sense of the nature and quality of research abroad and to find out whether the committee might learn something that is largely new to American researchers.

Members of the committee and staff visited Singapore and Germany in April and August, respectively. While the delegations were impressed with the quality of the research that they learned about during the site visits, they did not find completely novel approaches to the problems that the committee is addressing. This state of affairs is not surprising: Research has become so internationalized that most discussions and citations refer to multiple country sources. In several cases, even the funding for diverse projects comes from global sponsors. The differences are therefore more cultural than scientific and more relational than absolute. Consequently, what might be the most interesting about Germany and Singapore is how their approaches to research in human-machine collaboration and development differ from those of the United States and each other.[1]

Singapore focuses explicitly on applied research, technology transition, and commercialization. Its research teams—whether at Singapore's A*STAR (Agency for Science, Technology and Research) or in academia—are internationally integrated, with foreign nationals often holding the principal investigator position on a project. (Germany today is not so different in this respect. The DFKI [the German Research Centre for Artificial Intelligence], for example, has 154 researchers from 49 countries, with the largest number, 14, coming from China and the second largest, 13, from Russia.[2]) Singapore's main distinction, at least anecdotally, might be how it merges its emphasis on application and commercialization with an utterly globalized approach to research and development (R&D) to build itself into a global hub for science and technology. Thus, while Germany and the United States (and other countries that are centers of R&D excellence) might focus more on producing cutting-edge research, Singapore is unique in its commitment to becoming an essential go-to destination for the world's major industrial corporations.

As with Singapore, Germany also has a very strong commitment to applied research. Whereas Singapore explicitly relates their applied research to economic advancement, Germany focuses on the social aspect of applied research. For example, the Fraunhofer-Gesellschaft, the largest applied-research center in Europe, devotes their efforts "entirely to people's needs: health, security, communication, energy and the environment."[3]

Following are some of the highlights from the committee's trips abroad.

---

[1] See *S&T Strategies of Six Countries: Implications for the United States* (National Research Council, 2010).
[2] Overview of DFKI's Research Agenda, prepared for visit of CHMNI Delegation, August 1, 2013.
[3] See http://www.fraunhofer.de/en/about-fraunhofer.html. Last accessed February 10, 2014.

SINGAPORE, APRIL 15-19, 2013

A delegation traveled to Singapore for meetings on April 15–19 that focused on technologies related to human-machine collaboration for decision making. The institutions that the delegation visited span the spectrum between research (A*STAR and several universities) and application (such as the Defence Science Organisation and the Public Utilities Board). (The full list of institutions and brief descriptions of these visits can be found in this appendix).

Most of the technology that the delegation saw might not be considered cutting edge, although much of it is comparable to relevant efforts in the United States. Rather, one is struck by the breadth of this small country's R&D interests and the extent to which Singapore's scientists and technologists—regardless of national origin—exhibit a strong commitment to commercialize its research.

Two themes emerged consistently throughout the visit. The first, as described above, was the focus on applied research, technology transition, and commercialization. The pervasive message was that science and technology should serve business and industry. This principle was apparent at universities and research labs, and it led to strong efforts to develop industrial collaborations. It also contributed to the second theme, which was the development of international research collaborations and consortia and efforts to colocate researchers. The country aimed its scientific efforts not at basic research for the sake of knowledge acquisition, but at bringing people in, creating jobs, and/or inventing and improving technology.

The delegation spoke with several U.S. professors (by loan or direct hire) who, when pressed, revealed the benefits of working in Singapore. Topmost on their list was the freedom to pursue their research questions (typically advanced subjects that would push technological and privacy-related boundaries in the United States)—autonomous cars and social network research, for example (Singapore Management University and CREATE or the Campus for Research Excellence and Technological Enterprise). These professors also noted a particular type of collaboration setup spurred by the nature of Singaporean experimentation, with several universities and programs sharing a building on the same campus.

Singapore's style of governance allows the country to do some things relevant to this report's topic that would not be possible in the United States. In particular, it can achieve a high level of compliance in some areas that are considered personal choice in this country; similarly, Singapore's practices regarding respect for privacy are different from those exercised here. For example, all of the intersections with signals have sensors, as do highways. If a car breaks down, the system detects that the vehicle has pulled over and alerts traffic marshals. The intense monitoring not only facilitates service for the stranded motorist but also allows measurements of performance (such as how long it takes emergency crews to arrive) that can be used for assessment and future development. Similarly, all taxis contain sensors. Their movements allow larger traffic flow to be tracked.

As a result of these and related data-gathering activities, Singapore is positioned to be a leader in the new "data economy." Just as smart phones have stimulated a boom in cell-phone app development, large collections of new data might well prompt a flurry of innovation around how to use those data. Committee members suggested that Singapore is accumulating data in a more organized and comprehensive way than many other countries. This practice has a huge potential economic impact.

SINGAPORE VISIT SCHEDULE

April 15, Monday
AM: Nanyang Technological University: Centre for Computational Intelligence
PM: A*STAR: Institute for Infocomm Research (I^2R)

April 16, Tuesday
AM: CHMNI group discussion
PM: Dinner with a small group from the Symposium of Computational Intelligence, Cognitive Algorithms, Mind and Brain

April 17, Wednesday
AM: Defence Science Organization, Singapore
PM: A*STAR: Institute for High Performance Computing
Singapore Management University (LARC)

April 18, Thursday
AM: A*STAR: I^2R (Part 2)
PM: Site Visits to Public Utilities Board (flood control) and Land Transport Authority (traffic control)

April 19, Friday
AM: Singapore Institute for Neurotechnology (SINAPSE)
Singapore University of Technology and Design
PM: National Research Foundation
SMART Center (Singapore-MIT Alliance for Research and Technology)

GERMANY, August 1-3, 2013

The delegation visited DFKI, the German Research Centre for Artificial Intelligence, in Saarbrucken and Kaiserslautern on August 1; and the Fraunhofer Institute for Communication, Information Processing and Ergonomics, located in Wachtberg (a suburb of Bonn), on August 2. A committee member also met with Peter Hagoort in Berlin on August 3. Dr. Hagoort is director of the Max Planck Institute for Psycholinguistics, located in Njimgen, The Netherlands.

DFKI represents a private-public partnership of 16 companies, 3 universities, and 3 regional administrations that also receives funding from the Federal Ministry of Education and Research, the Federal Ministry of Economics and Technology, the German Research Foundation, and the European Union. They have 171 ongoing projects spread out among primarily four cities across Germany. These projects range from blue-sky research to commercialization in the area of software systems based on artificial intelligence. This institute does not have an obvious corollary in the United States. DFKI also hosts six "living labs" that house real equipment for advanced demonstrations in retail, advanced driver assistance, robotics, smart factories, smart cities, and ambient assistance.

Dr. Wolfgang Wahlster, director of DFKI, organized five presentations at DFKI in Saarbrucken and three more in Kaiserslautern. The presentations at Saarbrucken emphasized how computer-assisted technologies—from suggesting restaurants close by (called "choosability engineering") to stocking shelves, to driving and parking—can help with everyday life. The afternoon talks ranged from the "semantic desktop," a program that acts like a personal assistant, to real-time crowd monitoring, to body, hand, and object tracking; to 3-dimensional reconstruction under controlled conditions.

The next day, the delegation visited the Fraunhofer Institute for Communication, Information Processing and Ergonomics, or FKIE. This institute is part of Fraunhofer-Gesellschaft, an organization of 59 research institutes that conducts applied research for public and private enterprise and for social benefit. FKIE's research areas include unmanned systems, distributed information processing in heterogeneous systems, multisensor data fusion and ergonomics and human-machine systems. The delegation's host was Frank O. Flemisch, who directs the Department of Ergonomics and Human-Machine Systems. During this afternoon visit, FKIE researchers discussed and demonstrated several of their research projects, including human-machine interface design for command and control systems, methods and tools for human-machine integration, and cooperative vehicle control.

Both of the research institutes that the delegation visited are very interested in human-machine collaboration. Interestingly, much of the research explicitly seeks to mitigate technology overreliance. For example, if the computer-assist mechanism in a car does not experience human engagement for a period of time, it will ask whether the human wants to continue using the automatic system. It is possible that the social (as opposed to economic or defense) emphasis on research is an oblique reference to and refutation of Germany's past.

AGENDA for the VISIT to DFKI, SAARBRUKEN, and KAISERSLAUTEN

August 1, 2013

9:00 – 9:45	Introduction: Overview of DFKI's Research Agenda Prof. Dr. Wolfgang Wahlster, CEO, DFKI
9:45 – 10:10	Introduction to Choosability Engineering Prof. Dr. Anthony Jameson and Catalin Barbu
10:10 – 10:25	Parallel Exploration as a General Approach to Decision Support Prof. Dr. Anthony Jameson and Adrian Spirescu
10:25 – 10:40	Coffee break
10:40 – 11:00	A Situation-adaptive Multimodal Dialogue Platform for the Car Dr. Michael Feld
11:00 – 11:20	Process Mining as an Instrument for Decision Making in Organizations PD Dr. Peter Fettke
11:20 – 12:00	Agents and Semantics for Human Decision Making: Showcases and Challenges PD Dr. Matthias Klusch
12:00 – 12:15	Wrap-up
12:15 – 13:15	Lunch
13:15 – 14:15	Drive to Kaiserslautern
14:30 – 15:00	Decision Support for Knowledge Workers Prof. Dr. H. C. Andreas Dengel
15:00 – 15:45	Collaborative Social Sensing: New Human Machine Systems Dr. George Kampis
15:45 – 16:15	Video Analytics for User Support in Industrial and City Context Prof. Dr. Didier Stricker
16:15 – 16:30	Wrap-up

AGENDA for VISIT to FRAUNHOFER INSTITUTE

Visit of NRC at Fraunhofer FKIE Aug. 2nd, 2013

Patricia W. Wrightson, Katia Sycara

Frank Flemisch, Jessica Schwarz, Elena Dalinger et al.

Time	Presenter	Topic
13:00 – 13:30	Flemisch/NRC	Lunch
14:3o – 14:55	Flemisch	Introduction to Fraunhofer, FKIE, HSI
14:55 – 15:15	NRC	Overview of program
15:15 – 15:35	Dalinger	Assistant systems for security on civil ships
15:35 – 15:55	Schwarz	Workload assessment and assistant systems
16:00 – 16:30	Schwarz / Kaster	Demo Command & Control Center of the future
16:30 – 17:00	Heesen/Krasni	Demo Design Lab for Automation
16:30 – 17:00	All	Discussion on transatlantic scientific cooperation

Fraunhofer

Appendix C
REFERENCES

Bass, R. F. 1987. Computer-assisted observer training. *Journal of Applied Behavior Analysis*, 20(1):83–88.

Beck, A. H., Sangoi, A. R. Leung, S. Marinelli, R. J. Nielsen, T.O., va de Vijver, M. J. West, R. B., va de Rijn, M, and D. Koller. 2011. Systematic analysis of breast cancer morphology uncovers stromal features associated with survival. *Science Translational Medicine*, 3(108):108-113.

Benson, K., and S. Rotkoff. 2011. Goodbye, OODA loop. *Armed Forces Journal*, 26–41.

Berker A. O., M. Bikson, S. Bestmann. 2013. Predicting the behavioural impact of transcranial direct current stimulation: issues and limitations. *Frontiers of Human Neuroscience*.

Bradshaw, J. M., R. Hoffman, M. Johnson, and D. Woods. 2013. The seven deadly myths of "autonomous systems." *IEEE Intelligent Systems*, 28(3):54–61. doi:10.1109/MIS.2013.70.

Bradshaw, J. M., P. Feltovich, M. Johnson, M. Breedy, L. Bunch, T. Eskridge, H. Jung, J. Lott, A. Uszok, and J. van Diggelen. 2009. From tools to teammates: Joint activity in human-agent-robot teams. Human centered design. In *Lecture Notes in Computer Science*, vol. 5619, Masaki Kurosu, ed. Berlin, Germany: Springer, 935–944.

Bullard L.M., E. S. Browning, V. P. Clark, B. A. Coffman, C M. Garcia, R. E. Jung, A. J. van der Merwe, K. M. Paulson, A. A. Vakhtin, C. L. Wootton, M. P. Weisend. 2011. Transcranial direct current stimulation's effect on novice versus experienced learning.. *Exp Brain Res*. 2011 Aug;213(1):9-14. doi: 10.1007/s00221-011-2764-2. Epub 2011 Jun 26.

Casini E., J. Depree, N. Suri, J. M. Bradshaw, and T. Nieten. Enhancing decision-making by leveraging human intervention in large-scale sensor networks. *MILCOM* 2014, in press.

Christoffersen, K., and D. Woods. 2002. How to make automated systems team players. In *Advances in Human Performance and Cognitive Engineering Research*, vol. 2, E. Salas, ed. JAI Press/Emerald.

Clark, H., and S. Brennan. 1991. Grounding in communication. In *Perspectives on Socially Shared Cognition*, L. Resnick, J. Levine, and S. Teasley, eds. Washington, DC: American Psychological Association, 127–149.

Cooke, N. J., J. C. Gorman, C. W. Myers, and J. L. Duran. 2013. Interactive team cognition. *Cognitive Science*, 37(2):255–285. doi: 10.1111/cogs.12009.

Cooke, N. J., E. Salas, P. A. Kiekel, and B. Bell. 2004. Advances in measuring team cognition. In *Team cognition: Understanding the factors that drive process and performance*, E. Salas, S. M. Fiore, and J. A. Cannon-Bowers, eds. Washington, DC: American Psychological Association.

Crandall, J., and M. L. Cummings. 2007. Developing performance metrics for the supervisory control of multiple robots. *Proceedings of the ACM/IEEE International Conference on Human-Robot Interaction.* Washington, DC.

Cuevas, H. M., S. M. Fiore, B. S. Caldwell, and L. Strater. 2007. Augmenting team cognition in human-automation teams performing in complex operational environments. *Aviation, Space, and Environmental Medicine*; 78(5, Suppl.):B63–70.

Cummings, M. L. 2013. Man versus nachine. (under review 2014).

Cummings, M. L., and B. Donmez. 2013. Metrics for supervisory control system evaluation. *Oxford Handbook of Cognitive Engineering*, J. Lee and A. Kirlik, eds. New York, NY: Oxford University Press, 367–378.

Cummings, M. L., S. Bruni, and P. J. Mitchell. 2010. Human supervisory control challenges in network-centric operations. *Reviews of Human Factors and Ergonomics*, 6:34–78. doi:10.1518/155723410X12849346788660.

Defense Science Board. 2012. *Task Force Report: The Role of Autonomy in DoD Systems.* Office of the Under Secretary of Defense for Acquisition, Technology and Logistics: Washington, DC.

Dekker, S. W. A., and D. D. Woods. 2002. MABA_MABA or abracadabra? Progress in human-automation coordination. *Cognition, Technology & Work*, 4(4):240–244.

de Winter, J., and D. Dodou. 2014. Why the Fitts list has persisted throughout the history of function allocation. *Cognition, Technology & Work*, 16:1–11.

Donmez, B., P. E. Pina and M. L. Cummings. 2009. Evaluation criteria for human-automation performance metrics. In *Performance Evaluation and Benchmarking of Intelligent Systems*, R. Madhavan, E. Tunstel, and E. Messina, eds. New York: Springer Science+Business Media. doi:10.1007/978-1-4419-0492-8.

Dourish, P. 2001. *Where the Action Is: The Foundations of Embodied Interaction.* Cambridge, MA: MIT Press.

Entin, E. E., and E. B. Entin. 2001. Measures for evaluation of team processes and performance in experiments and exercises. *Proceedings of the 6th International Command and Control Research and Technology Symposium*, U.S. Naval Academy, Annapolis, MD.

Falk, E.B., M. B. O'Donnell, and M. D. Lieberman. 2012. Getting the word out: Neural correlates of enthusiastic message propagation. *Frontiers in Human Neuroscience*, 6:313.

Falk, E.B., E. T. Berkman, T. Mann, B. Harrison, and M. D. Lieberman. 2010. Predicting persuasion-induced behavior change from the brain. *Journal of Neuroscience*, 30: 8421-8424.

Fiore, S., and J. Schooler. 2004. Process mapping and shared cognition: Teamwork and the development of shared problem models. In *Team Cognition: Understanding the Factors that Drive Process and Performance*, E. Salas and S. Fiore, eds. American Psychological Association.

Fischhoff, B. 1975. Hindsight ≠ foresight: The effect of outcome knowledge on judgment under uncertainty. *Journal of Experimental Psychology: Human Perception and Performance*, 1:288–299.

Fishelson, M., and D. Geiger. 2002. Exact genetic linkage computations for general pedigrees. *Bioinformatics*, 18(12):s189-s198.

Fitts, P. M., ed. 1951. *Human Engineering for an Effective Air Navigation and Traffic Control System*. Washington, DC: National Research Council.

Flemisch, F, C. A. Adams, S. R. Conway, K. H. Goodrich, M. T. Palmer, and P. C. Schutte. 2003. *The H-Metaphor as a Guideline for Vehicle Automation and Interaction* (Report no. NASA/TM—2003-212672). Hampton, VA: NASA, Langley Research Center.

Forbes-Riley, K., and D. Litman. 2011. When does disengagement correlate with learning in spoken dialog computer tutoring? In *Artificial Intelligence in Education*, 22(2): 81–89.

Gal, Y., B. Grosz, S. Kraus, A. Pfeffer, and S. Shieber. 2010. Agent decision making in open mixed networks. *Artificial Intelligence*, 174(18):1460–1480.

Gerson, A. D., L. C. Parra, and P. Sajda. 2006. Cortically coupled computer vision for rapid image search. *IEEE Transactions on Neural Systems and Rehabilitation Engineering : A Publication of the IEEE Engineering in Medicine and Biology Society*, 14(2):174–179. doi:10.1109/TNSRE.2006.875550.

Gigerenzer, G. 2008. Why heuristics work. *Perspectives on Psychological Science*, 3(1):20-29.

Gigerenzer, G., P. M. Todd, and the ABC Research Group. 1999. *Simple Heuristics that Make Us Smart*. New York: Oxford University Press.

Gigerenzer, G., and D. G. Goldstein. 1996. Reasoning the fast and frugal way: Models of bounded rationality. *Psychological Review*, 103(4):650–669.

Grant, J., S. Kraus, and D. Perlis. 2005. Formal Approaches to Teamwork. In *We Will Show Them: Essays in Honor of Dov Gabbay*, vol. 2, S. Artemov, H. Barringer, A. S. d'Avila Garcez, L. Lamb, and J. Woods, eds. London: College Publications.

Grosz, B., and S. Kraus. 1996. Collaborative plans for complex group action. *Artificial Intelligence*, 86(2):269–357.

Hammond, J.S., R. L. Keeney, and H. Raiffa, 1999. *Smart Choices: A Practical Guide to Making Better Decisions*. Boston, MA: Harvard Business School Press.

Heckerman, D, Geiger, D, and Chickering, DM, Learning Bayesian Networks: The Combination of Knowledge and Statistical Data, Machine Learning. 1995. 20, p 197-243.

Hey, T., S. Tansley, and K. Tolle. 2009. *The Fourth Paradigm: Data-intensive Scientific Discovery*. Microsoft Research.

Hoffman, R. R., J. D. Lee, D. D. Woods, N. Shadbolt, J. Miller, and J.M. Bradshaw. 2009. The dynamics of trust in cyberdomains. *IEEE Intelligent Systems*, Nov/Dec: 5-11.

Hoffman, R. R., M. Johnson, J.M. Bradshaw, and A. Underbrink. 2013. Trust in automation. *IEEE Intelligent Systems*, 28(1):84-88.

Hollan, J., E. Hutchins, and D. Kirsh. 2000. Distributed cognition: Toward a new foundation for human-computer interaction research. *ACM Transactions on Computer-Human Interaction: Special Issue on Human-Computer Interaction in the New Millennium, Part 2*, 7(2):174–196.

Hollnagel, E., D. D. Woods, and N. Leveson, eds. 2006. *Resilience Engineering: Concepts And Precepts*. Aldershot, England, and Burlington, VT: Ashgate Publishing Company.

Hollnagel, E., and D. Woods. 2005. *Joint Cognitive Systems: Foundations of Cognitive Systems Engineering*. Boca Raton, FL: Taylor & Francis.

Horvitz, E. 1999. Principles of mixed-initiative user interfaces. *Proceedings of Special Interest Group on Computer-Human Interaction*.

Horvitz, E., C. Ruokanga, and S. A. Srinivas, and M. Barry. 1992. A Decision-Theoretic Approach to the Display of Information for Time-Critical Decisions: The Vista Project, In *Proceedings of SOAR-92*.

Howard, R.A., and J.E. Matheson, ed. Readings on the Principles and Applications of Decision Analysis. 1984. Menlo Park, CA: Strategic Decisions Group.

Hughes, G., S. Mathan, and N. Yeung. 2013. EEG indices of reward motivation and target detectability in a rapid visual detection task. *NeuroImage*, 64(1):590–600.

Hutchins, E. 1995. *Cognition in the Wild*. Cambridge, MA: MIT Press.

Itti, L., and C. Koch. Computational modelling of visual attention. 2001 *Nature Reviews Neuroscience*, 2(3):194-203.

Itti, L., G. Rees, and J. K. Tsotsos. 2005. *Neurobiology of Attention*, Burlington, MA: Academic Press.

Itti, L., and P. F. Baldi, A principled aproach to detecting surprising events in video. 2005. In: *Proc. IEEE Conference on Computer Vision and Pattern Recognition* (CVPR), Volume 1:631-637.

Jarrasse, N., V. Sanguineti, and E. Burdet. 2014. Slaves no longer: Review on role assignment for human–robot joint motor action. *Adaptive Behavior*, 22(1):70–82. doi:10.1177/1059712313481044.

Jennings, N. R., K. Sycara, and M. Wooldridge. 1998. A roadmap of agent research and development. *Autonomous Agents and Multi-Agent Systems*, 1(1):7–38.

Johnson, M., J.M. Bradshaw, P. J. Feltovich, C. M. Jonker, M. B. van Riemsdijk, and M. Sierhuis. 2014a. Coactive design: designing support for interdependence in joint activity. *Journal of Human-Robot Interaction*, 3(1):43-69.

Johnson, M., Bradshaw, J. M., Feltovich, P., Hoffman, R. R., and Woods, D. D. 2014b. The Seven Virtues of Effective Human-Machine Teamwork, *IEEE Intelligent Systems*, in press.

Kahneman, D. *Thinking, Fast And Slow*. 2011. New York, NY: Farrar, Straus and Giroux.

Keeney, R.L. 1992. *Value-Focused Thinking: A Path to Creative Decisionmaking*. Cambridge, MA: Harvard University Press.

Kinny, D., M. Ljungberg, A. S. Rao, E. Sonenberg, G. Tidhar, and E. Werner. 1994. Planned team activity. In *Artificial Social Systems - Selected Papers from the Fourth European Workshop on Modelling Autonomous Agents and Multi-Agent Worlds*,

MAAMAW-92 (Lecture Notes in Artificial Intelligence), C. Castelfranchi and E. Werner, eds. Heidelberg, Germany: Springer-Verlag 830, 227–256.

Kirsh, D. 2013. Embodied cognition and the magical future of interaction design. *ACM Transactions on Computer-Human Interaction*, 20(1). doi:http://dx.doi.org/10.1145/2442106.2442109.

Klein, G. A. 2008. Naturalistic decision making. *Human Factors*, 50(3):456–460.

Klein, G., B. M. Moon, and R. R. Hoffman. 2006a. Making sense of sensemaking: 1: alternative perspectives. *IEEE Intelligent Systems*, 21(4):70-73.

Klein, G., Brian M. Moon, and Robert R. Hoffman. 2006b. Making sense of sensemaking: 2: a macrocognitive model. *IEEE Intelligent Systems*, 21(5):88-91.

Klein, G., D. D. Woods, J. M. Bradshaw, R. R. Hoffman, and P. J. Feltovich. 2004. Ten challenges for making automation a 'team player' in joint human-agent activity. *IEEE Intelligent Systems*, 19(6):91-95.

Koller, D, and N. Friedman. 2009. *Probabilistic Graphical Models: Principles and Techniques*. Cambridge, MA: MIT Press.

Krizhevsky, A., I. Sustskever, and G. E. Hinton. ImageNet classification with deep convolutional neural networks. 2012. *Advances in Neural Information Processing* 25, Cambridge, MA: MIT Press.

Kruse, A.A. 2007. Operational neuroscience: neurophysiological measures in applied environments. *Aviat Space Environ Med.* 78(5), 4–191.

Law, E., and L. von Ahn. 2011. Human computation. *Synthesis Lectures on Artificial Intelligence and Machine Learning*, 5(3): 1-121. doi: 10.2200/S00371ED1V01Y201107AIM013

Lee, J., and N. Moray. 1994. Trust, self-confidence, and operators' adaptation to automation. *International Journal of Human-Computer Studies*, 40(1):153–184.

Levesque, H., P. Cohen, and J. Nunes. 1990. On acting together. *Proceedings of the Eighth National Conference on Artificial Intelligence*, 94–99.

Macdonald, J. S. P., S. Mathan, and N. Yeung. 2011. Trial-by-trial variations in subjective attentional state are reflected in ongoing prestimulus EEG alpha oscillations. *Frontiers in Psychology*, 2(82).

Manual, A. L., A. W. David, M. Bikson, A. Schnider. 2014. A. Frontal tDCS modulates orbitofrontal reality filtering. *Neuroscience* 264: 21-27.

Marshall, S. P. 2007. Identifying cognitive state from eye metrics. *Aviation, Space, & Environmental Medicine*, 78(5):165-175;

Marshall, S. P. 2007. Measures of attention and cognitive effort in tactical decision making. In M. Cook, J. Noyes, & V. Masakowski (Eds.), *Decision Making in Complex Environments* (321-332). Aldershot, Hampshire UK: Ashgate Publishing

Mathan, S., D. Erdogmus, C. Huang, M. Pavel, P. Ververs, J. Carciofini, M. Dorneich, and S. Whitlow. 2008. Rapid image analysis using neural signals. *CHI '08 Extended Abstracts on Human Factors in Computing Systems* (Florence, Italy, April 05–10, 2008). ACM, New York, NY, 3309–3314.

McKendrick, R., T. Shaw, E. de Visser, H. Saquer, B. Kidwell, and R. Parasuraman. 2014. Team performance in networked supervisory control of unmanned air vehicles: Effects of automation, working memory and communication. *Human Factors*, 56(3):463–475. doi:10.1177/0018720813496269.

Mercier, H., and D. Sperber. 2011. Why do humans reason? Arguments for an argumentative theory. *Behavioral and Brain Sciences*, 34(2):57–74.

Miller, A.C. 1976. *Development of Automated Aids for Decision Analysis*. Stanford Research Institute: Menlo Park, CA.

Miller, C. 2012. Frameworks for supervisory control: Characterizing relationships with uninhabited vehicles. *Journal of Human-Robot Interaction*, 1(2):183–201.

Moore, D.T. and R.R. Hoffman. Sensemaking: a transformative paradigm. 2011. *American Intelligence Journal*, 29(1):26-36.

Morrow, D. G., and U. M. Fischer. 2013. Communication in socio-technical systems. In *The Oxford Handbook of Cognitive Engineering*, J. Lee and A. Kirlik, eds. Oxford: Oxford University Press, 178–199.

National Research Council. 2013. *Frontiers in Massive Data Analysis*. Washington, DC: The National Academies Press.

National Research Council. 2014. *Emerging and Readily Available Technologies and National Security—A Framework for Addressing Ethical, Lethal and Societal Issues*. Washington, DC: National Academies Press.

National Research Council. 2014. *Autonomy Research for Civil Aviation: Toward a New Era of Flight*. Washington, DC: National Academies Press.

National Research Council. 2008. *Emerging Cognitive Neuroscience and Related Technologies*. Washington, DC: National Academies Press.

Nikolaidis, S., and J. A. Shah. 2013. Human-robot cross-training: Computational formulation, modeling and evaluation of a human team training strategy. *Proceedings of the 8th ACM/IEEE International Conference on Human Robot Interaction*, 33–40. doi:10.1109/HRI.2013.6483499.

Norman, D. A. 2013. *The Design of Everyday Things* (revised and expanded edition). New York; London: Basic Books; MIT Press (British Isles only).

Norman, D. A. 2007. *The Design of Future Things*. New York: Basic Books.

Norman, D. A. 1988. *The Psychology of Everyday Things*. New York: Basic Books.

Olsen, D. R., and M. A. Goodrich. 2003. *Metrics for Evaluating Human-Robot Interactions*. Presented at the Performance Metrics for Intelligent Systems, Gaithersburg, MD, 2003.

Oudiette, D., J. W. Antony, J. D. Creery, and K. A. Paller. 2013. The role of memory reactivation during wakefulness and sleep in determining which memories endure. *The Journal of Neuroscience*, 33(15):6672–6678.

Parasuraman, R., T. Sheridan, and C. Wickens. 2000. A model for types and levels of human interaction with automation. *IEEE Transactions on Systems, Man, and Cybernetics–Part A: Systems and Humans*, 30(2):286–297.

Parasuraman, R., and V. Riley. 1997. Humans and automation: Use, misuse, disuse, abuse. *Human Factors*, 39(2):230–253.

Pearl, J. 2009. *Causality: Models, Reasoning, and Inference*. 2nd Edition, Cambridge: Cambridge University Press.

Pearl, J. 1988. *Probabilistic Reasoning in Intelligent Systems: Networks of Plausible Inference*. San Mateo, CA: Morgan Kaufmann Publishers.

Pina, P. E., B. Donmez, and M. L. Cummings. 2008. *Selecting Metrics to Evaluate Human Supervisory Control Applications*. Cambridge, MA: MIT Humans and Automation Laboratory.

Pohlmeyer, E. A., J. Wang, D. C. Jangraw, B. Lou, S.-F. Chang, and P. Sajda. 2011. Closing the loop in cortically-coupled computer vision: A brain-computer interface for searching image databases. *Journal of Neural Engineering*, 8(3). doi:10.1088/1741-2560/8/3/036025.

Pritchett, A. R., S. Y. Kim, and K. M. Feigh, 2014. Modeling human–automation function allocation. *Journal of Cognitive Engineering and Decision Making*, 8(1)52-77. doi:10.1177/1555343413490944.

Qian, M., Mario Aguilar, Karen N Zachery, Claudio Privitera, Stanley Klein, Thom Carney, Loren W Nolte; Teledyne Scientific and Imaging LLC, Research Triangle Laboratory, Durham, NC 27713, USA. *IEEE transactions on bio-medical engineering* (Impact Factor: 2.15). 04/2009; 56(7):1929-37. DOI:10.1109/TBME.2009.2016670.

Quinn, A. J., and B. B. Bederson. 2011. Human Computation: A Survey and Taxonomy of a Growing Field. *CHI*, ACM 978-1-4503-0267-8/11/05.

Rasmussen, J. 1983. Skills, rules, and knowledge: Signals, signs, and symbols, and other distinctions in human performance models. *IEEE Transactions on Systems, Man, and Cybernetics*, 13(3):257–266.

Reason, J. T. 1990. *Human Error*. Cambridge, England; New York: Cambridge University Press.

Raiffa, H. 1968. *Decision Analysis: Introductory Readings on Choices Under Uncertainty*. Reading, MA: Addison-Wesley.

Raux, A., B. Langner, D. Bohus, A. W. Black, and M. Eskenazi. 2005. Let's go public! Taking a spoken dialog system to the real world. In *Proc. of Interspeech*.

Rickel, J., and W. Lewis Johnson. 2003. Extending virtual humans to support team training in virtual reality. In *Exploring Artificial Intelligence in the New Millennium*, G. Lakemeyer and B. Nebel, eds. San Francisco: Morgan Kaufmann Publishers.

Sajda, P., E. Pohlmeyer, J. Wang, L. C. Parra, C. Christoforou, J. Dmochowski, B. Hanna, C. Bahlmann, M. K. Singh, and Shih-Fu Chang. 2010. In a blink of an eye and a switch of a transistor: Cortically coupled computer vision. *Proceedings of the IEEE*, 98(3):462–478. doi:10.1109/JPROC.2009.2038406.

Salas, E., N. J. Cooke, and M. A. Rosen. 2008. On teams, teamwork, and team performance: discoveries and developments. *Human Factors*, 50(3):540–547.

Shachter, R.D. 1986. Evaluating influence diagrams. *Operations Research*, 34(6)(November-December):871-882.

Schmorrow, D. D., C. A. Bolstad, K. A. May, and H. M. Cuevas. 2012. Editors' introduction to the special issue on exploring cognitive readiness in complex operational environments: Advances in theory and practice, part I. *Journal of Cognitive Engineering and Decision Making*, 6(3):271–275.

Smith, P. J., E. McCoy, and C. Layton. 1997. Brittleness in the design of cooperative problem-solving systems: The effects on user performance. *IEEE Transactions on Systems, Man and Cybernetics*, 27(3):360–371.

Steinfeld, A., T. Fong, D. Kaber, M. Lewis, J. Scholtz, A. Schultz, and M. Goodrich. 2006. Common metrics for human-robot interaction. *HRI '06 Proceedings of the 1st ACM SIGCHI/SIGART Conference on Human-Robot Interaction*. ACM New York, NY, 33–40. doi:10.1145/1121241.1121249.

Stolcke, A., K. Ries, N. Coccaro, E. Shriberg, R. Bates, D. Jurafsky, P. Taylor, R. Martin, C. Van Ess-Dykema, and M. Meteer. Dialogue act modeling for automatic tagging and recognition of conversational speech. *Computational linguistics*, 26(3):339–373.

Sycara, K., and M. Lewis. 2004. Integrating agents into human teams. In *Team Cognition: Understanding the Factors that Drive Process and Performance*, E. Salas and S. Fiore, eds. American Psychological Association.

Tausczik, Y.R., and J.W. Pennebaker. 2013. Improving teamwork using real-time language feedback. *CHI*, ACM 978-1-4503-1899-0/13/04.

Todd, P. M., and G. Gigerenzer. 2007. Environments that make us smart: Ecological rationality. *Current Directions in Psychological Science*, 16(3):167–171. doi:10.1111/j.1467-8721.2007.00497.x.

Traum, D., J. Rickel, J. Gratch, and S. Marsella. 2003. Negotiation over tasks in hybrid human-agent teams for simulation-based training. *Proceedings of International Conference on Autonomous Agents and Multiagent Systems* (AAMAS).

Tversky, A, and D. Kahneman. 1974. Judgment under uncertainty: heuristics and biases. *Science*, 185(4157):1124-1131.

van Wissen, A., Y. Gal, B. A. Kamphorst, M. V. Dignum. 2012. Human-agent teamwork in dynamic environments. *Computers in Human Behavior*, 28(1): 23-33. doi: 10.1016/j.chb.2011.08.006.

Wildman, J. L., E. Salas, and P. R. Scott. 2013.Measuring cognition in teams: A cross-domain review. *Human Factors*, 20(10):1-31. doi:10.1177/0018720813515907

Woods, D. D., and M. Branlat. 2010. Hollnagel's test: Being "in control" of highly interdependent multi-layered networked systems. *Cognition, Technology & Work* 12(2):95-101. doi:10.1007/s10111-010-0144-5.

Woolley A. W., C. F. Cabris, A. Pentland., N. Hashmi, T. W. Malone. 2010. Evidence for a collective intelligence factor in the performance of human groups. *Science*, 330(6004):686-688; doi:10.1126/science.1193147.